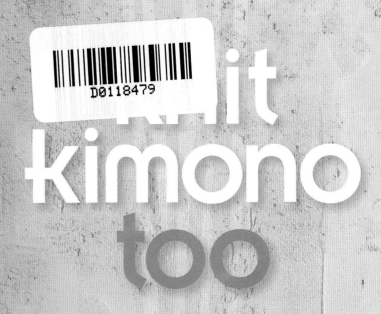

knit kimono too

simple designs
to mix, match + layer

VICKI SQUARE

INTERWEAVE
interweave.com

EDITOR Ann Budd

TECHNICAL EDITOR Karen Frisa

PHOTOGRAPHER Joe Hancock

PHOTO STYLIST Carol Beaver

HAIR + MAKEUP Kathy MacKay

TEXT ILLUSTRATIONS Vicky Square

ART DIRECTOR Liz Quan

COVER + INTERIOR DESIGN Pamela Norman

PRODUCTION Katherine Jackson

© 2010 Vicki Square

Photography © 2010 Interweave Press LLC

All rights reserved.

Interweave Press LLC
201 East Fourth Street
Loveland, CO 80537
interweave.com

Printed in China by Asia Pacific Offset Ltd.

Library of Congress Cataloging-
in-Publication Data

Square, Vicki, 1954-

Knit kimono too : simple designs to mix,
match, and layer / Vicki Square.

p. cm.

Includes index.

ISBN 978-1-59668-239-9 (pbk.)

1. Knitting--Patterns. 2. Kimonos. I. Title.

TT825.S713852 2010

746.43'2--dc22

2010012410

10 9 8 7 6 5 4 3 2 1

acknowledgments

For all who knit for beauty, and for those who appreciate it.

Arigatougozaimasu. Thank you all! I am humbled by the staggering sum of expertise all working in concert to build this book. My words here represent a small drop in the greater pool of heartfelt gratitude I have for each person who brought their part in this banquet of kimono beauty to the table.

Thank you to Tricia Waddell for believing in me to do this book, for her professional support of my vision, and to Marilyn Murphy and Interweave Book Group for getting behind this. Monumental thanks go to Ann Budd for her all-inclusive skills in superb editing, for her attention to detail, and her unflagging and ready encouragement in every aspect. To Liz Quan for her artistic vision and direction in combining the elements together beautifully for photo styling. To Karen Frisa for her expert and accurate technical editing and for making streamlined sense of my instructions. Thanks to Rebecca Campbell for her enthusiastic support while keeping me on task and on schedule.

Thank you to Joe Hancock for his extraordinary photography, displaying my designs with such an elegant aesthetic. And to the beautiful models who brought the kimono to life with such grace.

To my family of knitters, as always, I could not do this without you. I am grateful to you for coming alongside me in this work and for your many hours of excellent knitting. Sally Thieszen, Karen Tadich, Julie Richter, Sue Reynolds, Joan Pickett, Gina Kohler, Nancy Hewitt, Jeanne Fangman, Lois Eynon, and Allie Bush, you are without a doubt my foundation of friendship.

Thank you to all the yarn companies who graciously provided yarn of high quality, each chosen for its specific characteristics of beauty to enhance my designs. Berocco, Brown Sheep Company, Cascade Yarns, Classic Elite Yarns, Crystal Palace Yarns, Fiesta Yarns, Lana Grossa, Louet North America, Plymouth Yarn Company, Westminster Fibers/Rowan, Southwest Trading Company, and Tahki Stacy Charles, your exquisite yarns are a delight to work with.

Blessings to family, my husband Johnny, my son Alexander, and my daughter and son-in-law Justine and Jeffrey, for their constant support, encouragement, and prayers. You are all the light of my life. —*Vicki*

contents

color + kimono

I LOVE COLOR. Give me a color palette full of rich saturated colors, of soft muted heathers, of clear brights, of subtle shades, simple monochromatic schemes, complicated multicolor schemes . . . need I go on? Run the gamut, in other words.

In my second collection of knit kimono, I have focused on color, giving a brief nod to tradition and taking artistic license with shapes, textures, and finishing details. While the basic rectangular style is still very much in evidence, I offer a contemporary view of the eternal vogue of kimono. I have freely incorporated lace textures, slip-stitch color graphics, stranded color technique, and monochromatic knit/purl tactile designs. You will see square necklines, curved hems, button closures, and a unique scarf treatment.

Significant to this collection are the tops to layer underneath kimono. Any of the tops can be worn individually, but all are meant to accompany kimono in the color palette of your choice. Hence the title, *Knit Kimono Too.* I have designed sleeveless and short-sleeved varieties. They are of classic shape and coordinate well with the kimono in actual or visual texture. Most of all, the color of the tops can range from a classic expression of quiet neutrality to a burst of color that intensifies the kimono color statement.

Kimono in historical Japan had a stringent set of rules governing who could wear what colors in what fabric and at what time of year. Contemporary Japan, along with the rest of the world, throws the doors wide open to include all colors for all people. Aside from the black for mourning and the no-white-after-Labor-Day rules for America, both of which have been tossed, I am grateful that we have no boundaries for our color expression except for our own color aesthetic. Feel free to choose a palette that enhances your own personal coloring so that your clothing accentuates your natural beauty.

In the end, I invite you to be beautiful. I encourage you to personalize your color choices. I want you to feel like a million. Color is the most spectacularly dynamic way to achieve all these goals. Pursue them with enthusiasm!

a brief kimono history

KIMONO STYLE has evolved artistically over thousands of years. Subtle changes in shape have taken place, from the width of a kimono to the size of the sleeve opening. Fabrics changed continuously and no plant or animal fiber escaped notice. Bast fibers such as linen, hemp, and ramie, along with cotton, were primarily used by the common folk. Artisans in this social strata were masters in weaving and embellishing with simple tools and straightforward techniques. Functional as well as beautiful, these folk textiles have an unmatched depth of artistic character. For the royal court, silk in its various states of fineness was beautifully woven, either plain or in the richness of brocade. Silk was painted, dyed, embroidered, and in general manipulated with ever expanding achievements in technical skill.

Kimono was distilled from its Chinese influence to a fully Japanese aesthetic in the Heian period of history (794–1185). For 300 years spanning the end of the first millennium, nature-inspired color themes were orchestrated as visual art in clothing. Kimono was the canvas on which artists painted—literally or figuratively—their aesthetic visions.

The layering of colors was practiced to perfection, and what began as color sequences influenced by nature evolved into an elaborate list of colors dictated by tradition. Through this cultural process, distinct parameters were defined by which a person could display a personal sensibility of color nuance.

Color in kimono became known as definitive combinations called *irome no kasane*. Poetic names were given to color groupings that referred to nature's characteristics. Color names often derived from plant names or from a plant's dyeing properties, such as *kihada* (philodendron) for yellow, or for the color of a plant's blossom, such as *sakura* (cherry) for pale pink. Color names also referred to the affect of one color overlaid on another, called *awase-iro*—translucent white silk gauze over a dark green produces a frosty green called willow.

From the early to late Heian era, the basic apparel of noble ladies evolved from an opulent twelve to twenty layers of kimono to a more manageable layering of five robes, called *itsutsuginu*. Specific colors were named for each robe, its lining, and the unlined chemise or under *kosode*, and

figure 1

figure 2

figure 3

the entire set was then given a specific *kasane* name. The Senior Grand Empress Tashi of this era referred to a detailed manuscript that documented ensembles of named color sets in appropriate fabrics for each season of the year. This is the equivalent of a fashion consultant artistically coordinating all of your clothing and making a record of all the combinations so that there are no errors in your choices.

In a symphony of color, meaningful distinctions were defined. Major tones were produced by the outermost robe or robes. Minor tones gave counterpoint with the innermost chemise. Color accents occurred on middle robes or on linings. Color themes that were similar for different times of the year were made appropriate for the season through the fabric choices. Heavier, more densely woven fabrics for colder winter seasons and lighter, more open fabrics for hot summers provided the foundation for the seamless migration of color from season to season.

Some of the color sets from the closet of Empress Tashi are illustrated here as my interpretations of the color descriptions. Special occasion color palettes often used maroon (*suo*) as a major tone. All five robes could be a graduated shade of maroon, with a chemise of blue-green. One variation on this theme is three maroon robes from top or outer robe in order of dark, medium, and light, then a white robe followed by a deep persimmon colored inner robe. The inner chemise might offer a bright red as a counterpoint **(figure 1)**.

Arranging shades of one color in order of graduated value was known as *nioi*. Shades of sprout green (*moegi no nioi*) are layered from the lightest outer layer to the darkest inner layer, with a minor tone of scarlet pink as the chemise **(figure 2)**.

Among the most flamboyant color sets were those based on maple leaves. In a riotous combination of colors one recorded set of kasane colors began with a deep blue-green outer robe and progressed to a second robe of pale blue-green with a lining of scarlet pink. The third robe was pure yellow with a golden yellow lining followed by a fourth robe of golden yellow with a pure yellow lining. The fifth robe was scarlet pink with a pale yellow lining. The chemise was scarlet pink **(figure 3)**.

Plum themes offered major tones of pink with minor tones of green. One kasane shows pale pink as the top layer followed by light plum pink, then plum pink, then scarlet pink, with a maroon inner robe. The chemise uniquely is deep purple **(figure 4)**.

In a spectacularly commanding presentation of royalty, Empress Tashi could choose the forbidden color of deep purple

gradually lightening to a pale purple and finishing with white of the inner robes. As an undiluted color scheme, the chemise would be white **(figure 5)**.

While the meticulously recorded kasane of Empress Tashi is a standard in perpetuity, a simpler list of kimono colors from a traditional school of Japanese etiquette illustrates the rich transition of colors throughout the seasons. The January winter is reflected in pine green and deep purple. As the weather warms, crimsons of February lighten to peach in March. Clear and light summer colors begin with sprout green and yellow and end with cedar bark and sky blue. Autumn returns to vermillion and gray-green.

Even today, the nature-inspired Heian color sensibility is practiced throughout the world. We choose muted or saturated hues in dark shades for autumn and winter and light and fresh hues for spring and summer. There are not rules for how to use color, but there are exquisite examples of beautiful color arrangements. Creating a personal aesthetic can be as simple as following the lead of Japanese kimono color or as individual as observing nature's guidelines and choosing those colors that satisfy your soul.

figure 4

figure 5

roiyaru fusuma karaginu

FINISHED SIZE

About 44½" (113 cm) in circumference and 21" (53.5 cm) in length.

YARN

DK weight (#3 Light).

Shown here: Berroco Pure Pima (100% pima cotton; 115 yd [105 m]/50 g): #2227 sprout (green; MC), 10 skeins.

Berroco Mica (31% cotton, 26% silk, 23% nylon, 20% linen; 108 yd [99 m]/40 g): #1103 mushroom (beige; CC), 5 skeins.

NEEDLES

Body and sleeves: size U.S. 6 (4 mm): 24" (60 cm) circular (cir).
Edging: size U.S. 5 (3.75 mm): 24" (60 cm) cir and set of 2 double-pointed (dpn).

Adjust needle size if necessary to obtain the correct gauge.

NOTIONS

Stitch holders; removable markers; markers (m); three 1" (2.5 cm) buttons; safety pin; tapestry needle.

GAUGE

22 stitches and 40 rows = 4" (10 cm) in royal quilting pattern on larger needle; 22 stitches and 26 rows = 4" (10 cm) in stockinette stitch with MC on larger needle.

A *karaginu* is a short jacket of brocade, perhaps embroidered or painted, with relatively narrow sleeves. I juxtaposed this concept with the stunning quilted surface embroidery techniques common to working-class peasantry kimono. To avoid too much of a good thing, I limited the quilting stitch to the garment body and the sleeve cuffs. The result is a sophisticated little jacket to suit any occasion.

This kimono features an unusual square neckline that is mitered at the inside corners and faced for weight and stability. I detailed the front edge with attached knitted cord to provide a definitively Asian design element when the jacket is worn open and functional buttonholes when worn closed. The finishing work is time intensive for this kimono, but well worth the effort—the construction warrants couture designation.

stitch guide

ROYAL QUILTING
(multiple of 6 sts + 3)

ROW 1 (WS) With CC, k1, p1, *sl 5 pwise with yarn in back (wyb), p1; rep from * to last st, k1.

ROW 2 (RS) With MC, knit.

ROW 3 With MC, k1, purl to last st, k1.

ROW 4 With CC, k1, sl 3 pwise wyb, *insert right needle tip under loose strand of Row 1 and knit the next st while capturing the loose strand behind new st, sl 5 pwise wyb; rep from * to last 5 sts, k1 while capturing the loose strand of Row 1 as before, sl 3 pwise wyb, k1.

ROW 5 With CC, k1, sl 3 pwise wyb, *p1, sl 5 pwise wyb; rep from * to last 5 sts, p1, sl 3 pwise wyb, k1.

ROWS 6 AND 7 With MC, rep Rows 2 and 3.

ROW 8 With CC, k1, *knit the next st while capturing the loose strand of Row 5, sl 5 pwise wyb; rep from * to last 2 sts, k1 while capturing the loose strand of Row 5 as before, k1.

Repeat Rows 1–8 for pattern.

CENTERED DOUBLE DECREASE
Sl 2 sts tog kwise, k1, p2sso—2 sts dec'd.

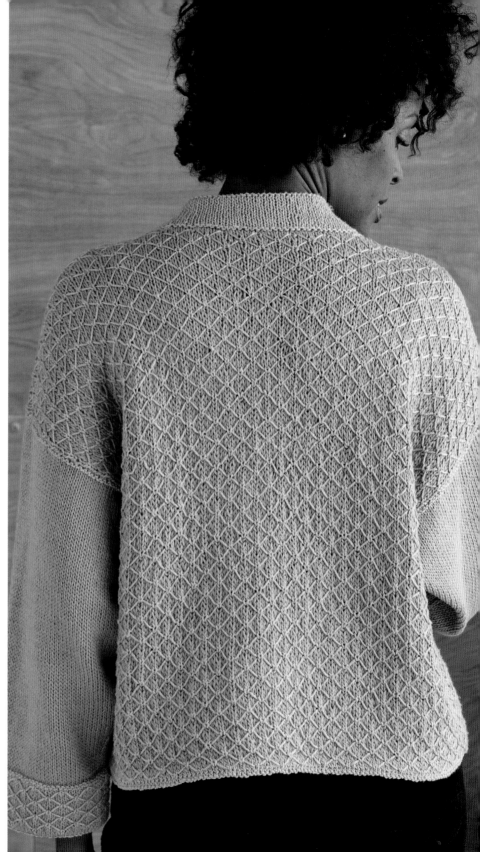

Back

With CC and larger needle, CO 123 sts. Do not join. Rep Rows 1–8 of royal quilting patt (see Stitch Guide) until piece measures 21" (53.5 cm) from CO, ending with Row 8 of patt. Place sts on holder.

Right Front

With CC and larger needle, CO 69 sts. Do not join. Rep Rows 1–8 of royal quilting patt until piece measures 14½" (37 cm) from CO, ending with Row 3 of patt. Cut off MC.

Shape Neck

(RS; Row 4 of patt) BO 24 sts kwise (do not slip any sts), capturing the loose strand as before in patt, work in patt to end—45 sts rem. Work 1 row in patt, then rejoin MC at neck edge and cont in patt until neck measures 6½" (16.5 cm), ending with Row 8 of patt. Place all sts on holder.

Left Front

With CC and larger needle, CO 69 sts. Do not join. Rep Rows 1–8 of royal quilting patt until piece measures 14½" (37 cm) from CO, ending with Row 4 of patt.

Shape Neck

(WS; Row 5 of patt) BO 24 sts (do not slip any sts), work in patt to end—45 sts rem. Cont in patt until neck measures 6½" (16.5 cm), ending with Row 8 of patt. Place all sts on holder.

Join Shoulders

Place 123 held back sts onto one needle and 45 held right front sts onto a second needle. With MC, larger needle, and RS tog, use the three-needle method (see Glossary) to BO 45 right front sts tog with 45 back sts for right shoulder, then BO next 33 sts for back neck, then

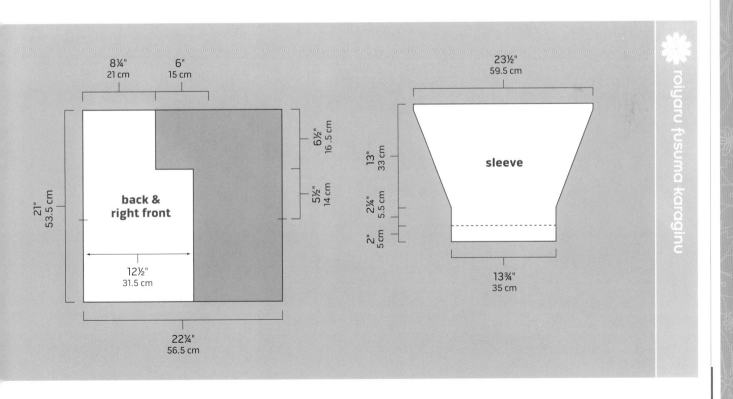

place 45 held left front sts onto a second needle and BO the 45 left front sts tog with 45 rem back sts for left shoulder. Wet-block (see Glossary) or lightly steam body flat. Let air-dry completely.

Sleeves

Measure down 12" (30.5 cm) from shoulder on front and back at side edge and mark for sleeve placement. With CC and smaller needle, pick up and knit 129 sts evenly between markers. Knit 1 (WS) row—1 garter ridge on RS. Change to MC and knit 1 row. Change to larger needle and purl 1 row. Dec 1 st each end of needle on next and every foll 3rd row 27 times total as foll:

RS ROWS K1, ssk, knit to last 3 sts, k2tog, k1—2 sts dec'd.

WS ROWS P1, p2tog, purl to last 3 sts, ssp (see Glossary), p1—2 sts dec'd; 75 sts rem when all decs have been worked. Work even until piece measures 13" (33 cm) from garter ridge, ending with a WS row. Change to CC and smaller needle and knit 3 rows, ending with a RS row—1 garter ridge on RS. Change to larger needle and work Rows 1–8 of royal quilting patt 2 times.

NEXT ROW (WS) With CC, k1, p1, *sl 5 pwise wyf, p1; rep from * to last st, k1. Change to smaller needle and, with CC, knit 2 rows—1 garter ridge on RS. Change to MC. Work in St st for 2" (5 cm) from garter ridge for facing. BO all sts.

Finishing

Neckband

With CC, smaller needle, RS facing, and beg at center right front, pick up and knit 24 sts along BO edge to inside corner, place marker (pm), 37 sts from corner to shoulder seam, 32 sts across back neck, 37 sts from left shoulder seam to corner, pm, and 24 sts along BO edge to center left front—154 sts total. Knit 1 (WS) row.

MITER SET-UP ROW K22, work a centered double dec (see Stitch Guide), removing m to work dec and replacing m after the dec is complete, knit to 1 st before next m, work a centered double dec, again removing m to work dec and replacing m after the dec, k22 to end—150 sts rem. Purl 1 (WS) row.

DEC ROW (RS) Knit to 2 sts before m, centered double dec, knit to 2 sts before next m, centered double dec, knit to end—4 sts dec'd. Purl 1 (WS) row. Rep the last 2 rows 3 more times—19 sts rem before first m and 18 sts rem after second m. Rep dec row once more—18 sts rem before first m and 17 sts rem after second m. Knit 1 (WS) row for garter turning ridge.

NEXT ROW (RS) K16, *k1f&b (see Glossary), k1 (center miter st), k1f&b*, knit to 2 sts before next m, rep from * to *, knit to end—4 sts inc'd. Purl 1 WS row.

INC ROW (RS) *Knit to 1 st before m, use the backward-loop method (see Glossary) to CO 1 st, k1 (center miter st), slip marker (sl m), CO 1 st as before; rep from * once, knit to end—4 sts inc'd. Purl 1 WS row. Rep the last 2 rows 3 more times, then work inc row once more—24 sts before first m. With WS facing, BO all sts pwise.

Seams

With MC threaded on a tapestry needle and using the mattress st with 1-st seam allowance (see Glossary) for body and ½-st seam allowance (see Glossary) for sleeve, sew side and sleeve seams. Fold sleeve facing to WS along garter turning ridge and, with MC threaded on a tapestry needle, whipstitch (see Glossary) into place, capturing one half of the BO st and the purl bar at the bottom of the first color change on the WS. With CC threaded on a tapestry needle, whipstitch neckband facing into place, capturing one half of the BO st of the neckband and BO edge of neckline.

Lower Edge

With CC, smaller needle, and RS facing, pick up and knit 1 st in each CO st along lower body edge—261 sts total. Knit 1 (WS) row for garter turning ridge. Change to MC and work in St st for 4 rows. BO all sts. Fold facing to WS of garment and, with MC, whipstitch in place, catching a purl bar and working loosely to avoid disturbing the RS of the work.

Center Right Front Edge

NOTE *Pick up and knit sts 1 full st in from the center front edge throughout, picking up about 2 sts for every 3 rows.*

With CC, smaller dpn, and RS facing, CO 4 sts. Holding needle with sts in right hand, work attached I-cord as foll: yo, pick up and knit 1 st in lower right front corner (working 1 st in from edge), pass the yo and the last CO st over the picked-up st, slide all 4 rem sts to other end of dpn.

NEXT ROW *K3, sl 1 kwise wyb, yo, pick up and knit 1 st in right front center edge, pass the yo and slipped st over the picked-up st, slide sts to other end of dpn.

Rep the last row for center edge of right front, picking up sts through both layers of neckband and facing and ending 1 row before aligning with upper neckband edge. BO all sts. Cut yarn and pull tail through rem st to secure.

Thread tail on a tapestry needle and sew to top edge of neckband, neatly joining top of I-cord beside neckband turning ridge.

Center Left Front Edge

Beg at upper edge of neckband, CO 4 sts and work attached I-cord as for right front for ¾" (2 cm) to middle of neckband. Work cord knot as described below.

Transfer the sts on the safety pin to the dpn and cont working attached I-cord for 4" (10 cm). Work cord knot again. Work attached I-cord for another 4" (10 cm). Work cord knot again, then cont working attached I-cord to 1 row from lower edge. BO all sts. Cut yarn and pull tail through last st to secure. Thread tail on a tapestry needle and sew to lower left front edge, neatly joining end of I-cord beside lower turning ridge.

Lightly steam front borders from WS and RS to set sts. Let air-dry completely. Sew buttons to right front, opposite cord knot buttonholes.

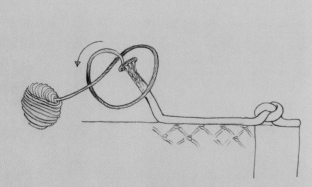

cord knot

Work regular (unattached) I-cord (see Glossary) for 3" (7.5 cm). Transfer the 4 sts onto a safety pin. Tie an overhand knot with the I-cord as foll: circle the cord and working yarn with the ball of attached yarn counterclockwise, then bring the ball of yarn through the loop. Follow with the cord until the full 3" (7.5 cm) of I-cord is used in the knot.

shimofuri chairo ke-bura

FINISHED SIZE

About 51½" (131 cm) in circumference—48¾" (124 cm) garment plus a 2¾" (7 cm) gap at center front—and 27½" (70 cm) in length.

YARN

Worsted weight (#4 Medium).

Shown here: Cascade Yarns Cascade 220 (100% wool; 220 yd [201 m]/100 g): #9539 brown marl (MC), 8 skeins; #9471 brown (CC), 1 skein.

NEEDLES

Size U.S. 8 (5 mm): two 29" (73.5 cm) circular (cir).

Adjust needle size if necessary to obtain the correct gauge.

NOTIONS

Cable needle (cn); waste yarn or stitch holders; removable markers; tapestry needle.

GAUGE

17 stitches and 25 rows = 4" (10 cm) in reverse stockinette stitch; 22 stitches and 26 rows = 4" (10 cm) in charted pattern.

Shizen iro, or natural color, describes the subtle *shibui* neutrals of brown and gray in the marled yarn I used for this kimono. The restrained *iki* style of subdued palette and barely visible woven patterns on the outside of kimono is brought front and center for this garment, which is at once cozy, comfortable, and classic. The overall cable pattern on the back and front panels defends the shape and the two-color garter slip-stitch pattern on the neckband and cuffs provides a statement of casual refinement.

Although only a small percentage of historical Japanese kimono fashion involved wool, its lure is too great for me to resist. For me, wrapping up in wool's soft warmth is a luxury that has become a standard.

stitch guide

GARTER SLIP-STITCH BORDER (multiple of 2 sts + 1)

NOTE Slip all sts purlwise.

ROWS 1 AND 2 With MC, knit.

ROW 3 (RS) With CC, k1, *sl 1 with yarn in back (wyb), k1; rep from *.

ROW 4 With CC, k1, *sl 1 with yarn in front (wyf), k1; rep from *.

ROWS 5 AND 6 With MC, knit.

ROW 7 With CC, k2, *sl 1 wyb, k1; rep from * to last st, k1.

ROW 8 With CC, k2, *sl 1 wyf, k1; rep from * to last st, k1.

Repeat Rows 1–8 for pattern.

Back

With MC, CO 142 sts. Do not join. Work Rows 14–16 of Back chart (see page 24) once, then rep Rows 1–16 until piece measures about 27½" (70 cm) from CO, ending with Row 16 of chart. Place sts on waste yarn holder.

Right Front

With MC, CO 51 sts. Do not join. Work Rows 14–16 of Right Front chart, then rep Rows 1–16 until piece measures about 27½" (70 cm) from CO, ending with Row 16 of chart. Place sts on waste yarn holder.

Left Front

With MC, CO 51 sts. Do not join. Work Rows 14–16 of Left Front chart, then rep Rows 1–16 until piece measures about 27½" (70 cm) from CO, ending with Row 16 of chart. Place sts on waste yarn holder.

Join Shoulders

Place 142 held back sts onto one needle and 51 held right front sts onto another needle. With RS tog, use the three-needle method (see Glossary) to BO 51 right front and back sts tog for right shoulder, then BO next 40 sts for back neck, then place 51 held left front sts onto second needle and use the three-needle method to BO 51 left front and rem back sts tog for left shoulder.

Sleeves

Measure and mark 13" (33 cm) down from shoulder on front and back at side edges. With MC and RS facing, pick up and knit 111 sts evenly spaced between markers. Do not join. Knit 3 rows. Change to rev St st (purl RS rows; knit WS rows) and work even until piece measures 1½" (3.8 cm) from pick-up row, ending with a WS row.

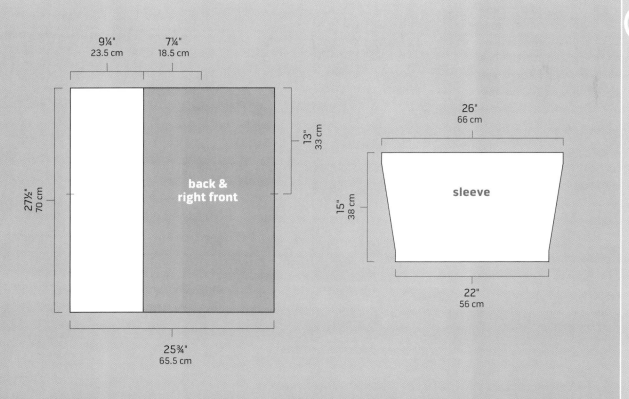

DEC ROW (RS) P1, ssp (see Glossary), purl to last 3 sts, p2tog, p1—2 sts dec'd. Work even in rev St st for 1½" (3.8 cm) ending with a WS row. Rep dec row. Dec 1 st each end of needle in this manner every 1½" (3.8 cm) 7 more times—93 sts rem. Knit 1 (WS) row. Work Rows 1–8 of garter slip-stitch border (see Stitch Guide) 2 times, then work Row 1 once more. With WS facing, BO all sts kwise.

Finishing

Neckband

With MC, RS facing, and beg at lower edge of right center front, pick up and knit 126 sts to right shoulder seam, 39 sts across back neck, and 126 sts from left shoulder seam to lower edge of left front—291 sts total. Working back and forth with 2 cir needles, knit 1 WS row. With CC and beg with Row 3, work through Row 8 of garter slip-stitch border, then work Rows 1–8 two more times, then work Row 1 once more— band measures about 2¼" (5.5 cm) from pick-up row. With WS facing, loosely BO all sts kwise.

Wet-block (see Glossary) to measurements. Let air-dry completely.

Seams

With MC threaded on a tapestry needle, RS facing, and using a mattress st for rev St st (see Glossary), sew side and sleeve seams, changing to mattress st for garter st (see Glossary) for cuffs. Lightly steam seams to set sts.

Right Front

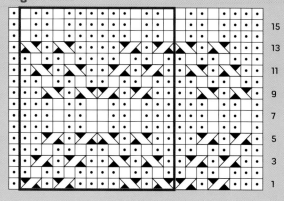

15
13
11
9
7
5
3
1

Left Front

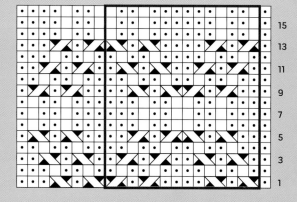

15
13
11
9
7
5
3
1

☐ k on RS; p on WS

· p on RS; k on WS

☐ pattern repeat

sl 1 st onto cn, hold in back, k1, p1 from cn

sl 1 st onto cn, hold in front, p1, k1 from cn

Back

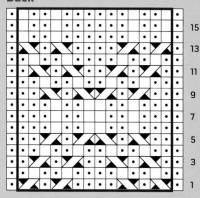

15
13
11
9
7
5
3
1

tsui-do hanten

FINISHED SIZE

About 38 (43, 48)" (96.5 [109, 122] cm) garment plus a 3" (7.5 cm) gap at center front, and about 24 (25, 26)" (61 [63.5, 66] cm) in length. Kimono shown measures 51" (129.5 cm).

YARN

Worsted and DK weight (#4 Medium and #3 Light).

Shown here: Tahki New Tweed (60% wool, 14% silk, 26% viscose; 92 yd [84 m]/50 g): #062 celery (MC), 14 (15, 16) balls.

Filatura di Crosa Brilla (42% cotton, 58% rayon; 120 yd [110 m]/50 g): #389 light yellow (CC), 1 ball.

NEEDLES

Body and sleeves: size U.S. 8 (5 mm): 24" (60 cm) circular (cir). *Bind-off:* size U.S. 8 (5 mm) or smaller spare needle. *Neckband:* size U.S. 7 (4.5 mm).

Adjust needle size if necessary to obtain the correct gauge.

NOTIONS

Stitch holders; tapestry needle.

GAUGE

20 stitches and 26 rows = 4" (10 cm) in 5/1 rib pattern with MC on larger needle.

Moegi is the name for the shade of green of delicate herb sprouts in the spring. Whether it is a pale blue-green or a green with yellow undertones, moegi is associated with clear and fresh greens. The pale celery green used for this *hanten*, a relatively short kimono, promises a lively harmony with essentially all other colors.

I used a simple 5/1 rib for the garment body and a 10/1 rib for the sleeves to create vertical textural stripes that will flatter any figure. The silk-wool tweed yarn is a matte counterpoint to the high gloss cotton of the surface embroidery—diagonal running stitches randomly spaced in the purl sections of the rib on the body. The front is meant to hang open to reveal the coordinating colors and textures underneath, whether casual or dressy.

stitch guide

5/1 RIB PATTERN (multiple of 6 sts + 5)

ROW 1 (RS) *P5, k1; rep from * to last 5 sts, p5.

ROW 2 *K5, p1; rep from * to last 5 sts, k5.

Repeat Rows 1 and 2 for pattern.

10/1 RIB PATTERN (multiple of 11 sts + 10)

ROW 1 (RS) *P10, k1; rep from * to last 10 sts, p10.

ROW 2 *K10, p1; rep from * to last 10 sts, k10.

Repeat Rows 1 and 2 for pattern.

NOTE *To test the gauge easily, cast on 29 sts and follow the 5/1 rib pattern for a few inches. Measure on the WS of work for easy counting of stitches.*

Back

With MC and larger needle, CO 103 (115, 127) sts. Do not join. Work 5/1 rib patt as foll:

ROW 1 (RS) P3, k1, *p5, k1; rep from * to last 3 sts, p3.

ROW 2 K3, p1, *k5, p1; rep from * to last 3 sts, k3.

Rep Rows 1 and 2 until piece measures 13 (14, 15)" (33 [35.5, 38] cm) from CO, ending with a WS row.

Shape Armholes

BO 2 sts at beg of next 2 rows—99 (111, 123) sts rem. Cont in patt as established until armholes measure 11" (28 cm), ending with a WS row. Place sts on holder.

Right Front

With MC and larger needle, CO 33 (39, 45) sts. Do not join. Work 5/1 rib patt as foll:

ROW 1 (RS) *P5, k1; rep from * to last 3 sts, p3.

ROW 2 K3, *p1, k5; rep from * to end.

Rep Rows 1 and 2 until piece measures 13 (14, 15)" (33 [35.5, 38] cm) from CO, ending with a RS row.

Shape Armhole

(WS) BO 2 sts, work in patt to end—31 (37, 43) sts rem. Cont in patt as established until armhole measures 11" (28 cm), ending with a WS row. Place sts on holder.

Left Front

With MC and larger needle, CO 33 (39, 45) sts. Do not join. Work 5/1 rib patt as foll:

ROW 1 (RS) P3, *k1, p5; rep from * to end.

ROW 2 *K5, p1; rep from * to last 3 sts, k3.

Rep Rows 1 and 2 until piece measures 13 (14, 15)" (33 [35.5, 38] cm) from CO, ending with a WS row.

Shape Armhole

(RS) BO 2 sts, work in patt to end—31 (37, 43) sts rem. Cont in patt as established until armhole measures 11" (28 cm), ending with a WS row. Place sts on holder.

Join Shoulders

Place 99 (111, 123) back sts onto one needle and 31 (37, 43) right front sts onto another needle. With MC, larger needle, and RS tog, use the three-needle method (see Glossary) to BO 31 (37, 43) right front and back sts tog for right shoulder, then BO next 37 sts for back neck, then place 31 (37, 43) left front sts onto second needle and BO 31 (37, 43) left front sts tog with rem back sts for left shoulder.

Sleeves

With MC, larger needle, RS facing, and beg at the corner of the armhole notch (not including the armhole BO sts), pick up and knit 54 sts evenly spaced along the armhole to the shoulder seam, 1 st

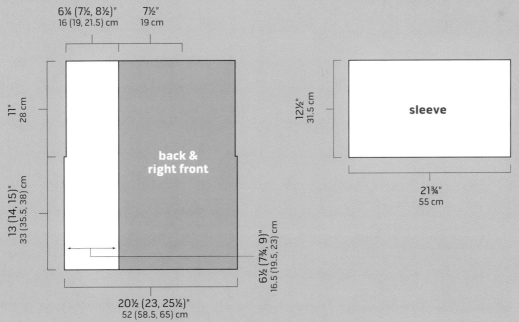

6¼ (7½, 8½)"
16 (19, 21.5) cm

7½"
19 cm

11"
28 cm

13 (14, 15)"
33 (35.5, 38) cm

**back &
right front**

6½ (7¾, 9)"
16.5 (19.5, 23) cm

20½ (23, 25½)"
52 (58.5, 65) cm

12½"
31.5 cm

sleeve

21¾"
55 cm

exactly in the shoulder seam, and 54 sts evenly spaced from the shoulder seam to the corner of the armhole notch—109 sts total. Do not join. Knit 1 row. Work 10/1 rib patt (see Stitch Guide) until piece measures 12" (30.5 cm) from pick-up row, ending with a WS row.

NEXT ROW (RS) Knit.

NEXT ROW *K10, p1; rep from * to last 10 sts, k10.

Rep the last 2 rows once more. Knit 1 row. BO all sts in patt.

Finishing

Wet-block (see Glossary) body to measurements. Let dry completely.

Seams

With MC threaded on a tapestry needle, sew side and sleeve seams using the mattress st for reverse St st and garter st (see Glossary) at cuff, working from RS, and sew top of sleeve seam to the 2 BO sts of front and back.

Neckband

With MC and smaller needles, CO 18 sts.

ROW 1 (WS) *K1, p1; rep from * to end.

ROW 2 (RS) Sl 1 with yarn in back (wyb), *p1, k1; rep from * to last st, p1.

Rep the last 2 rows until piece measures about 53 (55, 57)" (134.5 [139.5, 145] cm) from CO. Leave sts on needle.

Pin neckband onto garment, stretching band slightly to fit along first the right front edge, then across the back neck,

easing in any extra fullness, then along the left front edge. With MC threaded on a tapestry needle and beg at lower edge of right center front, use the mattress st for rev St st to sew band to garment, catching a purl st from the edge of the neckband and a corresponding purl st on the garment. Add or subtract band rows as necessary for a perfect fit. With RS facing, BO as foll: Sl 1 pwise, p1, BO 1 st, k1, BO 1 st, cont to BO in patt to end. Cut yarn and pull tail through last st to secure.

Embroidery

With a strand of CC 3 times the length of the garment body threaded on a tapestry needle and beg about ¾" (2 cm) below the shoulder seam and ending about ¾" (2 cm) above the bottom edge, work a diagonal and offset running stitch (see Glossary) 3 sts wide and 4 rows deep in the p5 rib sections as foll.

Right Front

Counting from right to left in each p5 section, bring needle from WS to RS in the 4th st, *bring needle diagonally down 4 rows and to the right 3 sts and insert the needle on the right-hand side of second st from RS to WS, then bring needle over to the 4th st and bring needle from WS to RS, 4 rows below the first insertion; rep from * to ¾" (2 cm) above lower edge, ending with needle on WS of fabric.

Left Front

Counting from right to left in each p5 section, bring needle from WS to RS to the right of the 2nd st, *bring needle diagonally down 4 rows and to the left 3 sts and insert the needle from RS to WS, then bring needle over to the 2nd st and bring needle from WS to RS, 4 rows below the first insertion; rep from * to ¾" (2 cm) above lower edge, ending with needle on WS of fabric.

Back

Work columns of diagonal and offset running st, angling each column as for left front or right front as shown in photo, or as desired.

Weave in loose ends. Lightly steam-block embroidery to set sts.

go-hitoe

FINISHED SIZE
About 49" (124.5 cm) in circumference and 25" (63.5 cm) in length.

YARN
Worsted weight (#4 Medium).

Shown here: Louet MerLin Worsted (70% merino, 30% linen; 156 yd [143 m]/100 g): #30 cream (MC), 9 skeins; #42 eggplant (A), #58 burgundy (B), #47 terra cotta (C), and #55 willow (D), 1 skein each.

NEEDLES
Body and sleeves: size U.S. 8 (5 mm): 24" (60 cm) circular (cir).
Edging: size U.S. 7 (4.5 mm): 24" (60 cm) cir.

Adjust needle size if necessary to obtain the correct gauge.

NOTIONS
Stitch holders; removable markers; tapestry needle.

GAUGE
17 stitches and 24 rows = 4" (10 cm) in stockinette stitch on larger needle.

Juni-hitoe, or twelve layers of kimono, was favored in Heian society (794–1192). The elaborate presentation of a color palette was determined foremost by rank and, perhaps secondarily, by season. Color guidelines were based on the cycles of nature and changes in the landscape. The sumptuary laws of the Edo Period (1600–1867) standardized the number of layers to five, or *go-hitoe*.

Heian layers revealed their colors at the front opening, lower hem, and sleeve cuff. Sometimes a final outer robe or ceremonial apron called a *mo* (commonly white) was added to formalize the ensemble. I did not adhere to strict rules of color set for this kimono but chose four colors that I admired in Japanese kimono and "topped" it with off-white.

Reverse stockinette-stitch bands highlight the color changes, and short-rows shape the colorwork at the center front. The yarn blend of merino and linen combines matte and shine that emulates tone-on-tone woven work.

stitch guide

**SEED STITCH
(even number of sts)**

ROW 1 (RS) *K1, p1; rep from *.

ROW 2 *P1, k1; rep from *.

Repeat Rows 1 and 2 for pattern.

**SEED STITCH
(odd number of sts)**

ALL ROWS *K1, p1; rep from *
to last st, k1.

Back

With MC and smaller needle, CO 104
sts. Do not join. Work in seed st (see
Stitch Guide) for 6 rows. Knit 1 row.
Change to larger needle and purl 1 WS
row. Cont in St st (knit RS rows; purl WS
rows) until piece measures 25" (63.5 cm)
from CO, ending with a WS row. Place
sts on holder.

Right Front

With MC and smaller needle, CO 45 sts.
Do not join. Work in seed st for 6 rows.
Knit 1 row. Change to larger needle
and purl 1 row. Cont in St st until piece

measures 5" (12.5 cm) from CO, ending
with a WS row.
DEC ROW (RS) K1, ssk, knit to end—1 st
dec'd.
Work 11 rows even in St st. Rep the
last 12 rows 6 more times—38 sts rem.
Work even until piece measures 25"
(63.5 cm) from CO, ending with a WS
row. Place sts on holder.

Left Front

With MC and smaller needle, CO 45 sts.
Do not join. Work in seed st for 6 rows.
Knit 1 row. Change to larger needle
and purl 1 row. Cont in St st until piece
measures 5" (12.5 cm) from CO, ending
with a WS row.
DEC ROW (RS) Knit to last 3 sts, k2tog,
k1—1 st dec'd.
Work 11 rows even in St st. Rep the
last 12 rows 6 more times—38 sts rem.
Work even until piece measures 25"
(63.5 cm) from CO, ending with a WS
row. Place sts on holder.

Join Shoulders

Place 104 held back sts onto one
needle and 38 held right front sts onto
another needle. With RS tog, use the
three-needle method (see Glossary) to
BO 38 right front sts tog with 38 back
sts for right shoulder, then BO next 28
sts for back neck, then place 38 held left
front sts onto another needle and use
the three-needle method to BO 38 left
front sts tog with rem 38 back sts for
left shoulder.

Sleeves

Measure down 16" (40.5 cm) from
shoulder on front and back at side edge
and mark for sleeve placement. With
D and smaller needle, pick up and knit
144 sts evenly spaced between markers.
Do not join. Knit 1 (WS) row—1 garter
ridge on RS. Change to MC and St st and
knit 1 row. Change to larger needle and
purl 1 row. Dec 1 st each end of needle
on next and every foll 3rd row 26 times
total as foll:
RS ROWS K1, ssk, knit to last 3 sts,
k2tog, k1—2 sts dec'd.
WS ROWS P1, p2tog, purl to last 3 sts,
ssp (see Glossary), p1—2 sts dec'd;
92 sts rem when all decs have been
worked.
Work even if necessary until piece
measures 13" (33 cm) from garter ridge,
ending with a WS row.
NEXT ROW (RS) Dec 8 sts evenly
spaced—84 sts rem.
Purl 1 row.

Cuff

Change to D and knit 2 rows, then purl
1 row, then knit 1 row, then purl 2 rows.
Change to MC and knit 1 row.
DEC ROW (WS) P1, p2tog, purl to last 3
sts, ssp, p1—2 sts dec'd.
Change to A and knit 2 rows, then purl
1 row, then knit 1 row, then purl 2 rows.
Change to MC and knit 1 row, then rep
dec row—80 sts rem. Change to B and
knit 2 rows, then purl 1 row, then knit
1 row, then purl 2 rows. Change to MC
and knit 1 row, then rep dec row—78 sts

rem. Change to C and knit 2 rows, then purl 1 row, then knit 1 row, then purl 1 row. With WS facing, BO all sts pwise.

Finishing

Neckband

With D, smaller needle, and RS facing, pick up and knit 102 sts along center right front edge, 29 sts across back neck, and 102 sts along center left front edge—233 sts total. Knit 1 WS row. Place the first 80 sts and the last 80 sts onto waste yarn holder—73 sts rem. Do not cut off D. Change to MC and knit 1 row. Slipping the first st of every row, work in seed st

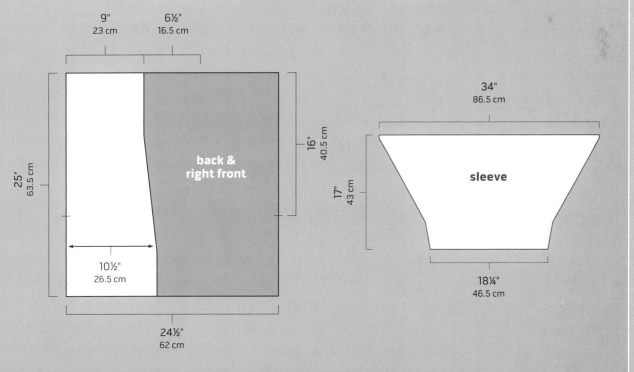

9"
23 cm

6½"
16.5 cm

back & right front

16"
40.5 cm

25"
63.5 cm

10½"
26.5 cm

24½"
62 cm

34"
86.5 cm

sleeve

17"
43 cm

18¼"
46.5 cm

until piece measures 1" (2.5 cm) from pick-up row, ending with a WS row.

DEC ROW Sl 1, work p2tog or k2tog as necessary to maintain patt, work in patt to end—1 st dec'd.

Rep dec row every row until collar measures 2½" (6.5 cm) from pick-up row, ending with a WS row. BO in patt as foll: sl 1, work p2tog or k2tog as necessary, BO 1 st, cont to BO in patt to last 3 sts, work p2tog or k2tog as necessary, BO 1 st, k1, BO 1 st. Pull cut end through last st to secure.

Right Front Color Layers

NOTE *When working short-rows, do not hide the wraps.*

Place 80 held right front sts onto smaller needle. With RS facing and D still attached, work short-rows (see Glossary) as foll:

SHORT-ROW 1 P70, wrap next st, turn, knit to end.

SHORT-ROW 2 P60, wrap next st, turn, knit to end.

SHORT-ROW 3 P50, wrap next st, turn, knit to end.

SHORT-ROW 4 Change to MC, k65, wrap next st, turn, purl to end.

NEXT 2 ROWS Change to A and knit 2 rows.

SHORT-ROWS 5–7 Rep Short-rows 1–3.

SHORT-ROW 8 Change to MC, k55, wrap next st, turn, purl to end.

NEXT 2 ROWS Change to B and knit 1 row, turn, slipping the first st, BO 5 sts, knit to end—75 sts rem.

SHORT-ROW 9 P65, wrap next st, turn, knit to end.

SHORT-ROW 10 P55, wrap next st, turn, knit to end.

SHORT-ROW 11 P45, wrap next st, turn, knit to end.

SHORT-ROW 12 Change to MC, k45, wrap next st, turn, purl to end.

NEXT 2 ROWS Change to C and knit 1 row, turn, slipping the first st, BO 5 sts, knit to end—70 sts rem.

SHORT-ROW 13 P60, wrap next st, turn, knit to end.

SHORT-ROW 14 P50, wrap next st, turn, knit to end.

SHORT-ROW 15 P40, wrap next st, turn, knit to end.

SHORT-ROW 16 Purl to last st, turn (1 st on right needle), slipping the next st, BO all sts kwise.

Left Front Color Layers

Place 80 held left front sts onto smaller needle. With WS facing, join D and work short-rows as foll:

SHORT-ROW 1 K70, wrap next st, turn, purl to end.

SHORT-ROW 2 K60, wrap next st, turn, purl to end.

SHORT-ROW 3 K50, wrap next st, turn, purl to end.

SHORT-ROW 4 Change to MC, p65, wrap next st, turn, knit to end.

NEXT 2 ROWS Change to A and purl 2 rows.

SHORT-ROWS 5–7 Rep Short-rows 1–3.

SHORT-ROW 8 Change to MC, p55, wrap next st, turn, knit to end.

NEXT 2 ROWS Change to B and purl 1 row, turn, slipping the first st, BO 5 sts, purl to end—75 sts rem.

SHORT-ROW 9 K65, wrap next st, turn, purl to end.

SHORT-ROW 10 K55, wrap next st, turn, purl to end.

SHORT-ROW 11 K45, wrap next st, turn, purl to end.

SHORT-ROW 12 Change to MC, p45, wrap next st, turn, knit to end.

NEXT 2 ROWS Change to C and purl 1 row, turn, slipping the first st, BO 5 sts, purl to end—70 sts rem.

SHORT-ROW 13 K60, wrap next st, turn, purl to end.

SHORT-ROW 14 K50, wrap next st, turn, purl to end.

SHORT-ROW 15 K40, wrap next st, turn, purl to end.

SHORT-ROW 16 Knit to last st, turn (1 st on right needle), slipping the next st, BO all sts pwise.

Seams

Weave in loose ends. With yarn threaded on a tapestry needle, use the mattress st with ½-st seam allowance (see Glossary) to sew side and sleeve seams, using mattress st for St st and rev St st (see Glossary) as necessary for sleeve cuffs.

Wash and Block

Machine-wash on gentle cycle using a non-bleach, mild soap. Place in dryer on a medium setting for 15 minutes, then lay flat to finish drying. Press gently with a warm iron, spreading out the front layers for shape.

ao

FINISHED SIZE

About 35 (39, 43, 47, 51)" (89 [99, 109, 119.5, 129.5] cm) in circumference and 20¼ (21¼, 23¼, 24¼, 25¼)" (51.5 [54, 59, 61.5, 64] cm) in length. Top shown measures 35" (89 cm).

YARN

Sportweight (#2 Fine).

Shown here: South West Trading Company Terra (50% bamboo, 50% cotton; 120 yd [110 m]/50 g): #449 azurite (green), 6 (6, 8, 9, 10) balls.

NEEDLES

Body: size U.S. 5 (3.75 mm): 24" (60 cm) circular (cir).
Edging: size U.S. 4 (3.5 mm): 24" (60 cm) cir.

Adjust needle size if necessary to obtain the correct gauge.

NOTIONS

Stitch holders; marker (m); tapestry needle.

GAUGE

22 stitches and 28 rows = 4" (10 cm) in stockinette stitch on larger needle.

Ao, one of the four oldest Japanese colors, is best described as blue-green. The vivid teal in this sleeveless top fits quite nicely into that ancient color spectrum (and enhances all skin tones). I designed this top to nip in at the waist for gentle shaping and a figure-flattering fit. The wide, shallow dancer neckline and lower hem feature a handsome traveling rib that also stabilizes the edges. The yarn is a combination of bamboo, which offers a soft hand and drape, and cotton, which retains the structure of the stitches.

The simple shape and subtle detail make this top ideal for layering, offering a pop of color that will enliven any kimono. Try it under the Tokai Tomoshibi (page 104) or choose your own styles and colors to mix and match.

stitch guide

RT (worked over 2 sts)
K2tog but leave the sts on the left needle tip, knit the first st again, then slip both sts off the left needle tip.

Back

With larger needle, CO 102 (113, 124, 135, 146) sts. Do not join. Work back and forth in rows as foll:

ROW 1 (RS) [K1, p1] 2 times, *[RT (see Stitch Guide)] 3 times, [p1, k1] 2 times, p1; rep from * to last 10 sts, [RT] 3 times, [p1, k1] 2 times.

ROWS 2 AND 4 [P1, k1] 2 times, *p6, [k1, p1] 2 times, k1; rep from * to last 10 sts, p6, [k1, p1] 2 times.

ROW 3 [K1, p1] 2 times, *k1, [RT] 2 times, k1, [p1, k1] 2 times, p1; rep from * to last 10 sts, k1, [RT] 2 times, k1, [p1, k1] 2 times.

Rep Rows 1–4 once more—8 rows total.

Change to St st (knit RS rows; purl WS rows) and work even until piece measures 2" (5 cm) from CO, ending with a WS row.

DEC ROW (RS) K1, k2tog, knit to last 3 sts, ssk, k1—2 sts dec'd.

Work 5 rows even in St st. Rep the last 6 rows 4 more times—92 (103, 114, 125, 136) sts rem. Work even until piece measures 8½ (9, 10, 10, 10½)" (21.5 [23, 25.5, 25.5, 26.5] cm) from CO, ending with a WS row.

INC ROW (RS) K1, use the backward-loop method (see Glossary) to CO 1 st, knit to last st, use the backward-loop method to CO 1 st, k1—2 sts inc'd.

Work even in St st until piece measures 10½ (11, 12½, 12½, 13)" (26.5 [28, 31.5, 31.5, 33] cm) from CO, ending with a WS row. Rep inc row—96 (107, 118, 129, 140) sts. Work even until piece measures 13 (13½, 15, 15½, 16)" (33 [34.5, 38, 39.5, 40.5] cm) from CO, ending with a WS row.

Shape Armholes

BO 3 sts at beg of next 2 rows, then BO 2 sts at beg of foll 2 rows—86 (97, 108, 119, 130) sts rem.

DEC ROW (RS) K1, k2tog, knit to last 3 sts, ssk, k1—2 sts dec'd.

Work 1 (WS) row even. Rep the last 2 rows 2 (6, 9, 12, 16) more times—80 (83, 88, 93, 96) sts rem. Work even until armholes measure 6 (6½, 7, 7½, 8)" (15 [16.5, 18, 19, 20.5] cm), ending with a WS row.

Shape Neck

Work short-rows (see Glossary) as foll:

Right Neck

SHORT-ROW 1 K28 (30, 33, 35, 37), wrap next st, turn, purl to end.

SHORT-ROW 2 K19 (20, 23, 25, 27), wrap next st, turn, purl to end.

SHORT-ROW 3 K11 (12, 15, 17, 19), wrap next st, turn, purl to end.

SHORT-ROW 4 K7 (7, 9, 11, 12), wrap next st, turn, purl to end.

SHORT-ROW 5 K4 (4, 6, 7, 7), wrap next st, turn, purl to end.

Cut off yarn.

Left Neck

Attach yarn to left armhole edge and, beg with a WS row, work as foll:

SHORT-ROW 1 P28 (30, 33, 35, 37), wrap next st, turn, knit to end.

SHORT-ROW 2 P19 (20, 23, 25, 27), wrap next st, turn, knit to end.

SHORT-ROW 3 P11 (12, 15, 17, 19), wrap next st, turn, knit to end.

SHORT-ROW 4 P7 (7, 9, 11, 12), wrap next st, turn, knit to end.

SHORT-ROW 5 P4 (4, 6, 7, 7), wrap next st, turn, knit to end.

Place all sts on smaller needle and set aside.

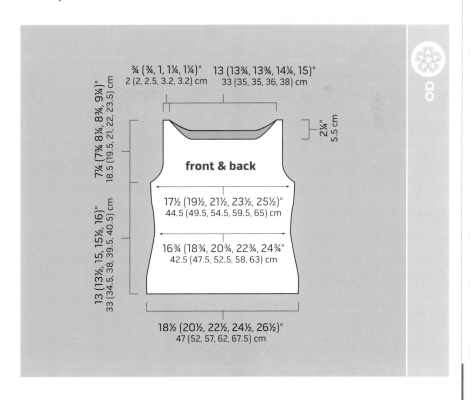

¾ (¾, 1, 1¼, 1¼)"
2 (2, 2.5, 3.2, 3.2) cm

13 (13¾, 13¾, 14¼, 15)"
33 (35, 35, 36, 38) cm

7¼ (7¾, 8¼, 8¾, 9¼)"
18.5 (19.5, 21, 22, 23.5) cm

2¼"
5.5 cm

front & back

17½ (19½, 21½, 23½, 25½)"
44.5 (49.5, 54.5, 59.5, 65) cm

16¾ (18¾, 20¾, 22¾, 24¾)"
42.5 (47.5, 52.5, 58, 63) cm

13 (13½, 15, 15½, 16)"
33 (34.5, 38, 39.5, 40.5) cm

18½ (20½, 22½, 24½, 26½)"
47 (52, 57, 62, 67.5) cm

Front

CO and work as for back until armholes measure 5 (5½, 6, 6½, 7)" (12.5 [14, 15, 16.5, 18] cm), ending with a WS row—80 (83, 88, 93, 96) sts rem.

Shape Neck
Work short-rows as foll:

Left Neck

SHORT-ROW 1 K30 (32, 34, 36, 38), wrap next st, turn, purl to end.

SHORT-ROW 2 K23 (24, 26, 28, 30), wrap next st, turn, purl to end.

SHORT-ROW 3 K17 (18, 20, 22, 23), wrap next st, turn, purl to end.

SHORT-ROW 4 K13 (14, 16, 18, 18), wrap next st, turn, purl to end.

SHORT-ROW 5 K10 (11, 13, 14, 14), wrap next st, turn, purl to end.

SHORT-ROW 6 K8 (8, 10, 11, 11), wrap next st, turn, purl to end.

SHORT-ROW 7 K6 (6, 8, 9, 9), wrap next st, turn, purl to end.

SHORT-ROW 8 K4 (4, 6, 7, 7), wrap next st, turn, purl to end.

Cut off yarn.

Right Neck

Attach yarn to right armhole edge and, beg with a WS row, work as foll:

SHORT-ROW 1 P30 (32, 34, 36, 38), wrap next st, turn, knit to end.

SHORT-ROW 2 P23 (24, 26, 28, 30), wrap next st, turn, knit to end.

SHORT-ROW 3 P17 (18, 20, 22, 23), wrap next st, turn, knit to end.

SHORT-ROW 4 P13 (14, 16, 18, 18), wrap next st, turn, knit to end.

SHORT-ROW 5 P10 (11, 13, 14, 14), wrap next st, turn, knit to end.

SHORT-ROW 6 P8 (8, 10, 11, 11), wrap next st, turn, knit to end.

SHORT-ROW 7 P6 (6, 8, 9, 9), wrap next st, turn, knit to end.

SHORT-ROW 8 P4 (4, 6, 7, 7), wrap next st, turn, knit to end.

Finishing

Join Shoulders

Hold back sts on one needle and front sts on another needle with RS tog. Use larger needle and the three-needle method (see Glossary) to BO 4 (4, 6, 7, 7) left front shoulder sts tog with 4 (4, 6, 7, 7) left back shoulder sts. Cut yarn and draw tail through rem st to secure. Rep for right shoulder—72 (75, 76, 79, 82) sts rem for each of front and back. Place sts on holder.

Weave in loose ends.

Armbands

With smaller needle and RS facing, pick up and knit 39 (42, 44, 47, 50) sts along front armhole, 1 st in the shoulder seam, and 39 (42, 44, 47, 50) sts along back armhole—79 (85, 89, 95, 101) sts total. Do not join.

NEXT ROW (WS) *P1, k1; rep from * to last st, p1.

With RS facing, BO all sts in k1, p1 rib as established.

Neck Edging

With smaller needle, RS facing, and working wraps tog with wrapped sts as you come to them, k72 (75, 76, 79, 82) front neck sts, pick up and knit 3 sts across the shoulder seam, k72 (75, 76, 79, 82) back neck sts, and pick up and knit 3 sts across other shoulder seam—150 (156, 158, 164, 170) sts total. Place marker (pm) and join for working in rnds.

Size 35" (89 cm) only

RND 1 *[RT] 3 times, [p1, k1] 2 times, p1*; rep from * to * 5 more times, [RT] 3 times, p2tog, k2tog, p2tog, k1, p1, rep from * to * 5 times, [RT] 3 times, p1, [k2tog, p2tog] 2 times—143 sts rem.

Size 39" (99 cm) only

RND 1 [RT] 3 times, p2tog, k2tog, p2tog, k1, p1, *[RT] 3 times, [p1, k1] 2 times, p1*; rep from * to * 3 more times, [RT] 3 times, p1, [k2tog, p2tog] 2 times, [RT] 3 times, p2tog, k2tog, p1, k1, p1, rep from * to * 5 times, [RT] 3 times, p1, [k2tog, p2tog] 2 times—143 sts rem.

Size 43" (109 cm) only

RND 1 [*[RT] 3 times, [p1, k1] 2 times, p1; rep from * 5 more times, [RT] 3 times, p1, k1, p1, k2tog, p2tog] 2 times—154 sts rem.

Size 47" (119.5 cm) only

RND 1 **[RT] 3 times, p2tog, k2tog, p1, k1, p1, *[RT] 3 times, [p1, k1] 2 times, p1; rep from * 4 more times, [RT] 3 times, p1, k1, p2tog, k2tog, p2tog; rep from ** once more—154 sts rem.

Size 51" (129.5 cm) only

RND 1 *[RT] 3 times, [p1, k1] 2 times, p1*; rep from * to * 6 more times, [RT] 3 times, p2tog, k2tog, p2tog, k1, p1, rep from * to * 6 times, [RT] 3 times, p1, k1, p1, k2tog, p2tog—165 sts rem.

All Sizes

RNDS 2 AND 4 *K6, [p1, k1] 2 times, p1; rep from *.

RND 3 *K1, [RT] 2 times, k1, [p1, k1] 2 times, p1; rep from *.

RND 5 *[RT] 3 times, [p1, k1] 2 times, p1; rep from *.

Rep Rnds 2 and 3 once more. BO all sts in patt.

Seams

With yarn threaded on a tapestry needle, use the mattress st with ½-st seam allowance (see Glossary) to sew side seams.

Steam- or wet-block (see Glossary) and let dry completely before moving.

inperiaru murasaki

FINISHED SIZE
About 38 (43½)" (96.5 [110.5] cm) in circumference and 23¼ (25¾)" (59 [65.5] cm) in length. Top shown measures 38" (96.5 cm).

YARN
Sportweight (#2 Fine).

Shown here: Louet MerLin Sport (60% wet-spun linen, 40% merino; 250 yd [229 m]/100 g): #45 violet (MC), 4 (5) skeins; #44 sandalwood (A) and #68 steel grey (B), 1 skein each.

NEEDLES
Size U.S. 2 (2.75 mm): 24" (60 cm) circular (cir) and extra needle the same size or smaller for three-needle bind-off.

Adjust needle size if necessary to obtain the correct gauge.

NOTIONS
Stitch holders; removable markers; two ¼" (6 mm) sew-on snaps; sewing needle and matching thread; tapestry needle.

GAUGE
24 stitches and 34 rows = 4" (10 cm) in stockinette stitch.

Purple, or *murasaki*, is a most universal color— a perfect foil for literally all other colors. Gromwell root, the source for murasaki dye, produced a wide range of purples. It was difficult to work with and was therefore reserved for royalty and those of high rank. With time, the initial saturation of the color tended to fade to a softer patina that was every bit as rich as its bold beginning.

The merino-linen blend I used for this kimono produces an exquisite knitted fabric that combines matte and shiny in a heathered texture. It recalls the aura of genteel aging. This slightly fitted sleeveless top has a stand-up collar and a Fair Isle band that defines a subtle curve from center front neck to right hip and hides a placket opening at the neck. The fine gauge yields a lightweight knitted fabric that is suitable for year-round wearing.

stitch guide

LINEN STITCH (panel of 8 sts)

ROW 1 (WS) [Sl 1 pwise wyb, p1] 3 times, sl 1 pwise wyb, k1.

ROW 2 (RS) Knit.

ROW 3 [P1, sl 1 pwise wyb] 3 times, p1, k1.

ROW 4 Knit.

Repeat Rows 1–4 for pattern.

Back

With MC, CO 134 (152) sts. Do not join. Work variation of linen st as foll:

ROW 1 (WS) P1, *sl 1 pwise with yarn in back (wyb), p1; rep from * to last st, p1.

ROWS 2 AND 4 Knit.

ROW 3 P2, *sl 1 pwise wyb, p1; rep from *.

Rep Rows 1–4 once more, then rep Rows 1–3 once again.

DEC ROW 1 (RS) *K7, ssk, k7, k2tog; rep from * 6 (7) more times, k8—14 (16) sts dec'd; 120 (136) sts rem.

Cont in St st (knit RS rows; purl WS rows) until piece measures 3 (4)" (7.5 [10] cm) from CO, ending with a WS row.

DEC ROW 2 (RS) K1, ssk, knit to last 3 sts, k2tog, k1—2 sts dec'd.

Work 5 rows even. Rep the last 6 rows 5 more times—108 (124) sts rem. Cont even until piece measures 10 (11)" (25.5 [28] cm) from CO, ending with a WS row.

INC ROW (RS) K1, right lifted increase in next st (RLI; see Glossary), knit to last st, left lifted increase (LLI; see Glossary), k1—2 sts inc'd.

Work 9 rows even. Rep the last 10 rows 2 more times—114 (130) sts. Cont even until piece measures 16 (17½)" (40.5 [44.5] cm) from CO, ending with a WS row.

Shape Armholes

BO 3 sts at beg of the next 2 rows, then BO 2 sts at beg of the foll 4 rows—100 (116) sts rem.

DEC ROW (RS) K1, ssk, knit to last 3 sts, k2tog, k1—2 sts dec'd.

Work 1 (WS) row even. Rep the last 2 rows 2 more times—94 (110) sts rem. Rep dec row every 4th row 6 times—82 (98) sts rem. Cont even until armholes measure 6¾ (7¾)" (17 [19.5] cm), ending with a WS row.

Shape Neck

(RS) K29 (36), BO 24 (26) sts, knit to end—29 (36) sts rem each side.

Left Neck

Purl 1 row. At neck edge, BO 9 sts, knit to end—20 (27) sts rem. Purl 1 row. Place sts on holder.

Right Neck

With WS facing, join yarn at neck edge. BO 9 sts pwise, purl to end—20 (27) sts rem. Work 2 rows even. Place sts on holder.

Front

CO and work as for back until armholes measure 2 (3)" (5 [7.5] cm), ending with a WS row.

Shape Placket and Neck

NOTE *Cont armhole shaping as established while working placket and neck shaping.* Place a removable marker before and after the center 8 sts to mark placket placement.

Left Side

Work to first m, remove m, place sts on left needle onto holder for right neck. Working back and forth on left neck sts only, work until armhole measures 4 (5)" (10 [12.5] cm), ending with a RS row. At neck edge (beg of WS rows), BO 5 sts once, then BO 3 sts 2 times, then BO 2 sts 2 times—22 (30) sts rem.

DEC ROW (RS) Knit to last 3 sts, ssk, k1—1 st dec'd.

Rep dec row every RS row 1 (2) more time(s)—20 (27) sts rem. Work even until armhole measures 7¼ (8¼)" (18.5 [21] cm). Place sts on holder.

Right Side

Place right neck sts onto needle. With RS facing, join yarn to neck edge. Work 1 (RS) row.

NEXT ROW (WS) Purl to m, work in linen st (see Stitch Guide) to end.

Cont in patt, working 8 sts at center front in linen st and rem sts in St st, until armhole measures 3¾ (4¾)" (9.5 [12] cm), ending with a WS row. At neck edge (beg of RS rows), BO 8 sts once, then BO 5 sts once, then BO 3 sts 2 times, then BO 2 sts 2 times—22 (30) sts rem. Work 1 (WS) row.

DEC ROW (RS) K1, k2tog, knit to end—1 st dec'd.

Rep dec row every RS row 1 (2) more time(s)—20 (27) sts rem. Work even until armhole measures 7¼ (8¼)" (18.5 [21] cm). Place sts on holder.

Finishing

Join Shoulders

Place 20 (27) sts for right back shoulder onto one needle and 20 (27) sts for right front shoulder onto another needle. With RS tog, use the three-needle method (see Glossary) to BO 20 (27) right front and back sts tog for right shoulder. Rep for left shoulder.

Armbands

With B, RS facing, and beg at base of armhole, pick up and knit 90 (102) sts along armhole edge. Do not join. Knit 1 row. Change to A and knit 1 row. With A and WS facing, BO all sts kwise.

Seams

With yarn threaded on a tapestry needle and using the mattress st with ½-st seam allowance (see Glossary), sew side seams.

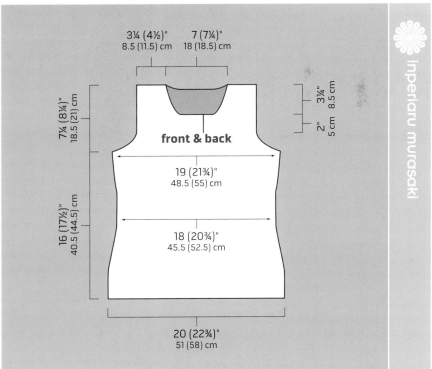

3¼ (4½)"
8.5 (11.5) cm

7 (7¼)"
18 (18.5) cm

3¼"
8.5 cm

2"
5 cm

7¼ (8¼)"
18.5 (21) cm

front & back

19 (21¾)"
48.5 (55) cm

16 (17½)"
40.5 (44.5) cm

18 (20¾)"
45.5 (52.5) cm

20 (22¾)"
51 (58) cm

imperiaru murasaki

Collar

With B and beg after placket on right front neck edge, pick up and knit 24 sts along right front neck edge, 42 (44) sts across back neck, and 24 sts along left front neck edge—90 (92) sts total. Knit 1 (WS) row. Change to A and knit 1 row.

ROWS 1, 5, AND 7 (WS) Sl 1 pwise with yarn in front (wyf), *sl 1 pwise wyb, p1; rep from * to last st, p1.

ROWS 2, 4, AND 8 Sl 1 kwise wyb, knit to end.

ROWS 3, 9, 11, 13, AND 15 Sl 1 pwise wyf, *p1, sl 1 pwise wyb; rep from * to last st, p1.

ROWS 6, 10, 12, 14, AND 16 Sl 1 kwise wyb, k2tog, knit to last 3 sts, ssk, k1—2 sts dec'd; 80 (82) sts rem after Row 16.

ROW 17 Sl 1 pwise wyf, knit to last st, p1—1 garter ridge on RS.

Facing

ROW 1 Sl 1 kwise wyb, use the backward-loop method (see Glossary) to CO 1 st, knit to last st, use the backward-loop method to CO 1 st, k1—2 sts inc'd.

ROW 2 Sl 1 pwise wyf, purl to end.

Rep the last 2 rows 2 more times—86 (88) sts. Slipping the first st of every row as established, cont in St st until facing measures the same length as the collar, ending with a WS row. BO all sts. Fold collar at garter ridge with WS tog.

With A threaded on a tapestry needle, whipstitch (see Glossary) facing to WS. To secure layers tog, work a running st (see Glossary) along each end of collar inside the slipped edge sts.

Weave in loose ends. Steam-press garment with iron set for linen. Let cool completely before moving.

Fair Isle Curved Band

With A and leaving a 3 (3¼) yd (2.7 [3] m) tail, use the long-tail method (see Glossary) to CO 168 (184) sts. Working the first 2 and last 2 sts in garter st (knit every row) with A, work the center 164 (180) sts according to Rows 1–13 of Fair Isle chart. With A, k2, purl to last 2 sts, k2. With RS facing, BO all sts pwise. Cut yarn, leaving a 36 (38)" (91.5 [96.5] cm) tail for seaming.

Press band from front and back, steaming heavily. Let cool completely before moving.

Beg just below collar, pin band onto front of garment, attaching only to left front to base of placket, then attaching both edges straight down from neck for about 3" (7.5 cm) below lower edge of placket, then curving toward right hip, ending at bottom of side seam with selvedge edge of band aligning with CO edge of front. With CO tail threaded on a tapestry needle, whipstitch band in place as invisibly as possible, catching 1 strand of CO edge and leaving the garter ridge evident. Rep for BO tail and BO edge.

With sewing needle and matching thread, sew prong side of each snap to WS of Fair Isle band—one at the corner and the other 1" (2.5 cm) below the first along the BO edge. Sew the other sides of snaps to linen-st edge of placket.

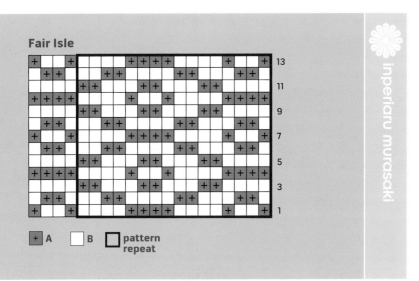

Fair Isle

+ A ☐ B ☐ pattern repeat

nagai uwagi

FINISHED SIZE

About 51½" (131 cm) in circumference and 42" (106.5 cm) in length.

YARN

Chunky and worsted weight (#5 Bulky and #4 Medium).

Shown here: Brown Sheep Company Lanaloft Handpaint Bulky (100% wool; 160 yd [146 m]/200 g) #BLL111 purple iris (MC), 10 skeins.

Lanaloft Bulky (100% wool; 160 yd [146 m]/200 g) #BLL82 deep violet (A), 3 skeins.

Lanaloft Worsted (100% wool; 160 yd [146 m]/100 g) #LL82W deep violet (B), 1 skein.

NEEDLES

Body and sleeves: size U.S. 11 (8 mm) 24" (60 cm) circular (cir).
Edging: size U.S. 10½ (6.5 mm) 24" (60 cm) cir.

Adjust needle size if necessary to obtain the correct gauge.

NOTIONS

Removable markers (m); large stitch holders; waste yarn in a contrasting color; tapestry needle; size H/8 (5 mm) crochet hook.

GAUGE

13 stitches and 26 rows = 4" (10 cm) in horizontal herringbone pattern with MC on larger needle.

In dramatic fashion, this long coat kimono provides winter warmth in a single layer that accommodates all the clothing worn beneath. For this design, I chose a herringbone slip-stitch pattern to produce a firm fabric that will retain its shape, and I knitted two-layer cuffs to emulate the many layers of robe typical of court attire during the Heian period. Cuffs in successively smaller circumference function both to keep out the cold and to hold the sleeves in place. For a unique closure treatment, I attached a shaped scarf on one side that pulls through a slot in the opposite front and hangs in lovely bias folds. The subtle blend of purples and grays in this bulky handpainted yarn is classic and tasteful.

While the Heian court ladies may have looked spectacular in their twelve to twenty layers of kimono robes, you'll find movement is much easier in this *uwagi*.

stitch guide

**HORIZONTAL HERRINGBONE
(multiple of 4 sts + 2)**

ROW 1 (RS) K2, *sl 2 pwise with yarn in front (wyf), k2; rep from *.

ROW 2 P1, *sl 2 pwise with yarn in back (wyb), p2; rep from * to last st, p1.

ROW 3 Sl 2 wyf, *k2, sl 2 wyf; rep from *.

ROW 4 P3, *sl 2 wyb, p2; rep from * to last 3 sts, sl 2 wyb, p1.

ROWS 5–12 Rep Rows 1–4 two times.

ROW 13 Rep Row 3.

ROW 14 Rep Row 2.

ROW 15 Rep Row 1.

ROW 16 Rep Row 4.

ROWS 17–24 Rep Rows 13–16 two times.

Repeat Rows 1–24 for pattern.

Body

With MC and smaller needle, CO 182 sts. Do not join. Work even in St st until piece measures 2" (5 cm) from CO, ending with a WS row. Purl 2 rows—1 garter ridge on RS. Change to larger needle and rep Rows 1–24 of horizontal herringbone patt (see Stitch Guide) until piece measures 8" (20.5 cm) from garter ridge, ending with a WS row.

DEC ROW (RS) K2tog, work in patt to last 2 sts, k2tog—2 sts dec'd.

NOTE *Dec on WS rows by working p2tog at each end of needle if it is easier to maintain patt continuity.*

Rep dec row when piece measures 16" (40.5 cm), 20" (51 cm), 24" (61 cm), and 28" (71 cm) from garter ridge—172 sts rem. Work even until piece measures 29" (73.5 cm) from garter ridge, ending with a WS row.

Divide for Fronts and Back

Keeping in patt, work 38 sts for right front and place these sts on a holder, BO 12 sts for right armhole, work 72 sts for back, BO 12 sts for left armhole, work to end for left front and place these 38 sts on holder—38 held sts for each front; 72 sts for back. Do not cut yarn.

Back

With WS facing, join MC to 72 back sts and cont in patt until armholes measure 11" (28 cm), ending with a WS row. Place sts on waste yarn holder.

Right Front

Place 38 right front sts onto larger needle. With WS facing, join MC and cont in patt until armhole measures 3" (7.5 cm), ending with a WS row.

Shape Neck

DEC ROW (RS) K2tog, work in patt to end—1 st dec'd.

Work 3 rows even. Rep the last 4 rows 11 more times—26 sts rem. Work even in patt until armhole measures 11" (28 cm), ending with a WS row. Place all sts on waste yarn holder.

Left Front

Place 38 left front sts onto larger needle. With WS facing and using MC already attached, cont in patt until armhole measures 3" (7.5 cm), ending with a WS row.

Shape Neck

DEC ROW (RS) Work in patt to last 2 sts, k2tog—1 st dec'd.

Work 3 rows even. Rep the last 4 rows 11 more times—26 sts rem. Work even in patt until armhole measures 11" (28 cm), ending with a WS row. Place all sts on waste yarn holder.

Sleeves

With MC and larger needle, CO 74 sts. Do not join. Purl 1 row. Work Rows 1–24 of horizontal herringbone patt 3 times, then work Rows 1–23 once more. Change to smaller needle and work Row 24—piece measures about 14¾" (37.5 cm) from CO. Change to A and knit

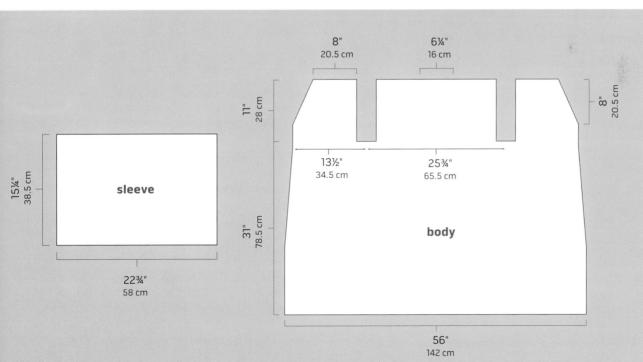

sleeve

15¼"
38.5 cm

22¾"
58 cm

8"
20.5 cm

6¼"
16 cm

11"
28 cm

8"
20.5 cm

13½"
34.5 cm

25¾"
65.5 cm

body

31"
78.5 cm

56"
142 cm

2 rows. BO all sts. Cut yarn, leaving a tail about 3 yd (2.7 m) long for seaming.

First Cuff Layer

With A and larger needle, CO 50 sts. Do not join.

ROW 1 (WS) *K2, p2; rep from * to last 2 sts, k2.

ROW 2 *P2, k2tog through back loop (k2togtbl; see Glossary) and leave these sts on left needle, k2tog as usual through the fronts of the same sts, then drop both sts from left needle; rep from * to last 2 sts, p2.

ROW 3 *K2, p1, yo, p1; rep from * to last 2 sts, k2.

ROW 4 *P2, ssk, k1; rep from * to last 2 sts, p2.

ROWS 5 AND 6 Rep Rows 1 and 2.

ROW 7 Rep Row 1.

With RS facing, BO all sts in patt.

Second Cuff Layer

With MC and larger needle, CO 41 sts. Do not join.

ROW 1 (WS) *P1, k1; rep from * to last st, p1.

ROW 2 (RS) *K1, p1; rep from * to last st, k1.

Rep Rows 1 and 2 three more times—8 rows total. With WS facing, BO all sts in patt.

Scarf

With B and smaller needle, CO 13 sts.

Row 1 (WS) Sl 2 pwise wyf, p9, sl 2 pwise wyf.

ROW 2 (RS) Knit.

Rep Rows 1 and 2 until piece measures 5" (12.5 cm) from CO, ending with a WS row.

INC ROW (RS) K2, right lifted inc (RLI; see Glossary) in next st, knit to last 2 sts, left lifted inc (LLI; see Glossary), k2—2 sts inc'd.

Work 3 rows even, working all WS rows as foll: sl 2 pwise wyf, purl to last 2 sts, sl 2 pwise wyf.

Rep the last 4 rows 19 more times—53 sts. Work short-rows (see Glossary) to shape lower edge as foll:

SHORT-ROW 1 K2, RLI, work to last 7 sts, wrap next st, turn, purl to last 2 sts, sl 2 pwise wyf—54 sts.

SHORT-ROW 2 Work to 5 sts before previously wrapped st, wrap next st, turn, purl to last 2 sts, sl 2 pwise wyf.

SHORT-ROW 3 K2, RLI, work to 5 sts before previously wrapped st, wrap next st, turn, purl to last 2 sts, sl 2 pwise wyf—1 st inc'd.

Rep Short-rows 2 and 3 three more times, then work Short-row 2 once more—58 sts. Knit 1 (RS) row across all sts, working wraps tog with wrapped sts.

NEXT ROW (WS) Sl 2 pwise wyf, knit to last 2 sts, sl 2 pwise wyf.

NEXT ROW Knit.

Slipping the first 2 sts pwise wyf, BO to the last 2 sts, p2tog, then BO last st. Cut yarn and pull through rem st to secure.

Finishing

Weave in loose ends.

Blocking

Wrap body, sleeves, cuffs, and scarf in wet towels, up to, but not including, rolled hem on body. Place rolled bundle in large plastic bag overnight to achieve uniform dampness. Lay out flat to measurements. Let air-dry completely.

Join Shoulders

Place 72 held back sts onto one needle and 26 held right front sts onto another needle. With MC, RS tog, and larger needle, use the three-needle method (see Glossary) to BO 26 right front and 26 back sts tog for right shoulder, BO next 20 sts for back neck, then place 26 held left front sts onto another needle and use the three-needle method to BO 26 left front and rem 26 back sts tog for left shoulder. Cut yarn and pull through last st to secure.

Front Border

With A and larger needle, CO 21 sts.
ROW 1 (RS) K10 for facing, sl 1 pwise wyb for fold line, k10 for border.
ROW 2 Purl.
Rep Rows 1 and 2 until piece measures about 86" (218.5 cm) from CO, or the length needed to extend from lower right front edge, across back neck, and to lower left front edge. BO all sts.

Beg at lower right front edge, pin outer layer of front border to body from lower right front edge, across back neck, and down to lower left front edge, stretching very slightly to prevent ripples. With A threaded on a tapestry needle, use the mattress st with a ½-st seam allowance (see Glossary) to sew border (not facing) to body, leaving 3" (7.5 cm) unsewn on the left front from 7" to 10" (18 to 25.5 cm) down from the shoulder. Fold the border along the slipped-st column and with A threaded on a tapestry needle, use a whipstitch (see Glossary) to sew facing in place on WS, leaving 3" (7.5 cm) unsewn as before.

Seams

With RS tog, pin BO edge of sleeve to armhole, matching center of BO edge to shoulder seam and matching corners of sleeve to corners at base of armhole. With tail of A, WS facing, and working from the sleeve side, use slip-st crochet (see Glossary) to join the sleeve to the body from armhole corner to armhole corner. Turn RS out. Mark center of armhole BO. With MC and using the mattress st, sew sleeve from each corner to center of BO, then sew sleeve seam from underarm to cuff.

With A threaded on a tapestry needle, use mattress st for rev St st with ½-st seam allowance to sew selvedge edges of first cuff layer tog. With MC threaded on a tapestry needle, use mattress st with ½-st seam allowance (see Glossary) to sew selvedge edges of second cuff layer tog. Mark center of each cuff.

With A threaded on a tapestry needle and RS of first cuff facing WS of sleeve, use a whipstitch to sew BO edge of the first cuff to WS of lower sleeve, aligning centers and underlapping the cuff about 1" (2.5 cm) so that the eyelet rib is visible and beg and ending the seam about 1" (2.5 cm) from the cuff selvedge seam (2" [5 cm] of cuff will rem free). Whipstitch the RS of the second cuff to the WS of the first cuff, aligning centers and leaving about 1" to 1½" (2.5 to 3.8 cm) unsewn at each side of cuff selvedge seam (2" to 3" [5 to 7.5 cm] of cuff will rem free).

With B threaded on a tapestry needle, use a whipstitch to sew CO edge of scarf to right front border about 4" (10 cm) down from the shoulder.

Weave in loose ends. Lightly steam scarf seam and front border seam to set sts.

nishiki

FINISHED SIZE

About 47½" (120.5 cm) in circumference and 33" (84 cm) in length.

YARN

Worsted weight (#4 Medium).

Shown here: Cascade Venezia Worsted (70% merino, 30% silk; 219 yd [200 m]/100 g): #158 egg-plant (A), 8 skeins; #170 blue (B), 6 skeins.

NEEDLES

Size U.S. 8 (5 mm): two 29" (73.5 cm) circular (cir).

Adjust needle size if necessary to obtain the correct gauge.

NOTIONS

Stitch holders; size F/5 (3.75 mm) crochet hook; waste yarn for pro-visional CO; removable markers; tapestry needle.

GAUGE

22 stitches and 22 rows = 4" (10 cm) in stockinette stitch, worked in charted pattern.

Eggplant and cobalt; murasaki and ao; purple and blue. Deep and saturated for winter; pale and clear for summer. However you describe these colors, they are a rich combination that beautifully represents the brocade, or *nishiki*, inference of the overall Fair Isle pattern.

For this kimono, I used a curvilinear pattern on the main garment pieces and a strong geometric pattern to border and balance the design. The shaped front panels cause the lower hem to sweep from the side up to the center front overlap. The sleeves sweep from underarm to cuff to further emphasize the dramatic curves. The neckband, lower hem, and sleeve cuffs are all faced to offer weight and stability.

With its soft hand, this wool-silk blend yarn is the perfect weight and smooth texture to emulate the padded silks worn during the colder half of the year. Purple symbolizes royalty; blue can signify fidelity. Together the colors harmoniously dignify this traditionally influenced—yet completely con-temporary—kimono.

Back

With A and using the crochet chain method (see Glossary), provisionally CO 130 sts. Do not join. Purl 1 WS row. Beg and ending as indicated for back, work Rows 1–12 of Motif chart (see opposite page) 14 times, then work Rows 1 and 2 once more—piece measures about 31" (78.5 cm) from CO. Place sts on holder.

Right Front

With A and using the crochet chain method, provisionally CO 70 sts. Do not join.

Shape Lower Edge

Work Right Front chart while working short-rows (see Glossary) as foll:

SHORT-ROW 1 (WS) Work Row 1 of chart, wrap next st, turn work.

SHORT-ROW 2 Work Row 2 of chart.

SHORT-ROW 3 Working wrap tog with wrapped st as you come to it, work Row 3 of chart, wrap next st with both colors (hold both strands in one hand and wrap as one strand), turn work.

SHORT-ROW 4 Work Row 4 of chart. Cont as charted, reading chart shaping as short-rows and hiding wraps when you come to them, through Row 23 of chart—piece measures about 4¼" (11 cm) from CO at side edge. Beg and ending as indicated for right front, work Rows 11 and 12 of Motif chart once, then work Rows 1–12 of chart once, then work Rows 1 and 2 once more—piece measures about 7" (18 cm) from CO at side edge.

Right Front

22
20
18
16
14
12
10
8
6
4
2
(WS)

Left Front

23
21
19
17
15
13
11
9
7
5
3
1

nishiki

Motif

11
9
7
5
3
1

end left front
beg right front
beg back
end right front
beg sleeve; end sleeve
end back
beg left front

A

B

□ pattern repeat

Edging

11
9
7
5
3
1

end cuff
beg border
end neckband
beg sleeve
end sleeve
end neckband
end border
beg cuff

59

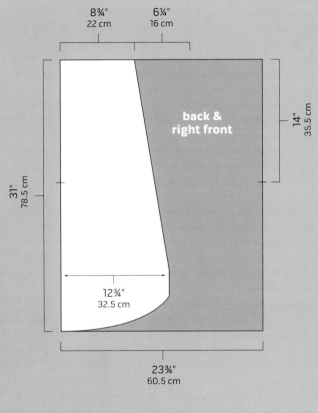

8¾"
22 cm

6¼"
16 cm

back &
right front

14"
35.5 cm

31"
78.5 cm

12¾"
32.5 cm

23¾"
60.5 cm

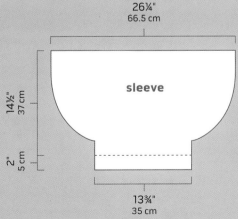

26¼"
66.5 cm

sleeve

14½"
37 cm

2"
5 cm

13¾"
35 cm

Shape Neck

DEC ROW (RS) K2tog, work in patt to end—1 st dec'd.

Work 5 rows even in patt. Rep the last 6 rows 21 more times—48 sts rem. Place sts on holder.

Left Front

With A and using the crochet chain method, provisionally CO 70 sts. Do not join. Purl 1 row.

Shape Lower Edge

Work Left Front chart while working short-rows as foll:

SHORT-ROW 1 (RS) Work Row 1 of chart, wrap next st with both yarns, turn work.

SHORT-ROW 2 Work Row 2 of chart.

SHORT-ROW 3 Working wrap tog with wrapped st as you come to it, work Row 3 of chart, wrap next st with both colors, turn work.

Cont as charted, reading chart shaping as short-rows and hiding wraps when you come to them, through Row 24 of chart—piece measures about 4½" (11.5 cm) from CO at side edge. Beg and ending as indicated for left front, work Rows 1–12 of Motif chart once, then work Rows 1 and 2 once more—piece measures about 7" (18 cm) from CO at side edge.

Shape Neck

DEC ROW (RS) Work in patt to last 2 sts, ssk—1 st dec'd.

Work 5 rows even in patt. Rep the last 6

rows 21 more times—48 sts rem. Place sts on holder.

Join Shoulders

Place 130 held back sts onto one needle and 48 held left front sts onto another needle. With WS tog, use A and the three-needle method (see Glossary) to BO 48 left front and 48 back sts tog for left shoulder, then BO the next 34 back sts as usual, then place 48 held right front sts onto second needle and BO 48 right front sts tog with rem 48 back sts for right shoulder.

Sleeves

Measure and mark 14" (35.5 cm) down from each shoulder on both front and back at side edge. With B and RS facing, pick up and knit 144 sts evenly spaced between markers (picking up a st exactly in the shoulder seam to avoid a hole). Knit 1 WS row. Beg and ending as indicated for sleeve, work Rows 1–12 of Edging chart. With B, knit 2 rows. Beg and ending as indicated for sleeve, work Rows 1–4 of Motif chart.

DEC ROW K2tog, work in patt to last 2 sts, ssk—2 sts dec'd.

Rep dec row every 4th row 4 more times, then every 2nd row 4 times—126 sts rem. Cont in patt, BO 2 sts at beg of next 14 rows—98 sts rem. BO 3 sts at beg of next 2 rows, then BO 4 sts at beg of foll 4 rows—76 sts rem. With B, knit 2 rows. Beg and ending as indicated for cuff, work Rows 1–12 of Edging chart. Knit 2 rows with B—1 garter ridge on RS. Cut off B. Change to A and work even in St st

for facing until piece measures 2" (5 cm) from garter ridge. BO all sts.

Finishing

Steam- or wet-block (see Glossary) garment flat in one layer for ease in finishing work. Let air-dry completely before moving.

Seams

With A threaded on a tapestry needle, use the mattress st with 1-st seam allowance (see Glossary) to sew side and sleeve seams. Fold cuff facing to WS along garter ridge and whipstitch (see Glossary) the edge half of the BO sts to the WS, catching the purl sts in the row just above cuff.

Lower Border

Carefully remove waste yarn from provisional CO of right front, back, and left front and place exposed sts onto needle—270 sts total. With RS facing and B, knit 1 row, working k2tog at each "seam"—268 sts rem. With B and working back and forth with 2 cir needles, knit 1 WS row. Beg and ending as indicated for border, work Rows 1–12 of Edging chart. With B, knit 2 rows for turning ridge. Cut off B. Change to A and work in St st until piece measures 2" (5 cm) from turning ridge. BO all sts.

Neckband

With B and beg at garter ridge on lower right front edge, pick up and knit 148 sts along right front, 34 sts across back neck, and 148 sts along left front, ending at garter ridge on lower left front

edge—330 sts total. With B and working back and forth with 2 cir needles, knit 1 WS row. Beg and ending as indicated for neckband, work Rows 1–12 of Edging chart. With B, knit 2 rows for turning ridge. Cut off B. Change to A and work in St st until piece measures 2" (5 cm) from turning ridge. BO all sts.

Steam-block lower border and neckband. Let air-dry completely before moving. Fold lower border facing to WS along garter turning ridge and whipstitch in place on WS, catching the purl sts in the row just above lower border and the edge half of the BO sts. Fold neckband facing to WS along garter turning ridge and whipstitch in place, catching the seam allowance sts from the pick-up row and the edge half of the BO sts. Whipstitch neckband facing to lower border facing.

Neckband Edging

With B and crochet hook, work single crochet (sc; see Glossary) along lower edge of neckband, securing the two layers tog as you go.

Weave in loose ends. Steam-block seams and edge treatments to set sts.

re-su katabira

FINISHED SIZE
About 45 (55½)" (114.5 [141] cm)
in circumference and 27 (30¾)"
(68.5 [78] cm) in length. Kimono
shown measures 45" (114.5 cm).

YARN
DK weight (#3 Light).

Shown here: Berroco Mica (31%
cotton, 26% silk, 23% nylon, 20%
linen; 108 yd [99 m]/40 g): #1126
jarosite (yellow), 12 (15) skeins.

NEEDLES
Body and sleeves: size U.S. 9
(5.5 mm): 24" (60 cm) circular (cir).
Edging: size U.S. 7 (4.5 mm): 24"
(60 cm) cir.

Adjust needle size if necessary
to obtain the correct gauge.

NOTIONS
Stitch holders; tapestry needle.

GAUGE
15 stitches and 21 rows = 4" (10 cm)
in charted lace pattern on larger
needle.

The ocher of this *katabira,* a thin morning kimono, is a cross between *kuchiba*—a subdued tan—and *yamabuki*—a golden yellow reminiscent of the common freesia. The color emphasizes lightness and the openwork reveals under layers and interacts for an integrated color palette. For a bold color scheme, pair this with the dark eggplant Suo Amanuno (page 76); dead-leaf yellow and purple are a color combination for May, according to a traditional Japanese calendar. For a softer look, pair it with the natural white Shiro Shiriku (page 110) or the Under Kosode Shell (page 126).

I chose an undulating diamond lace pattern for the back and front panels and a checkerboard of lace and solid squares for the sleeves. Garter stitch stabilizes the fluidity of the open-work pattern at the neckband and cuffs. Press the finished piece to intensify the drape for a truly luxurious kimono to wear any time of the day or night.

Back

With larger needle, CO 83 (103) sts. Do not join.

ROW 1 (WS) *P1, k1; rep from * to last st, p1.

ROW 2 *K1, p1; rep from * to last st, k1.

SET-UP ROW (WS) P1, right lifted inc in next st (RLI; see Glossary), purl to end—84 (104) sts.

Work Rows 1–20 of Lace chart (see page 68) until piece measures about 27 (30¾)" (68.5 [78] cm) from CO, ending with Row 20 of chart. Knit 2 rows—1 garter ridge on the RS. Place all sts on holder.

Right Front

With larger needle, CO 33 (43) sts. Do not join.

ROW 1 (WS) *P1, k1; rep from * to last st, p1.

ROW 2 *K1, p1; rep from * to last st, k1.

SET-UP ROW (WS) P1, right lifted inc in next st, purl to end—34 (44) sts.

Work Rows 1–20 of Lace chart until piece measures about 27 (30¾)" (68.5 [78] cm) from CO, ending with Row 20 of chart. Knit 2 rows—1 garter ridge on RS. Place all sts on holder.

Left Front

With larger needle, CO 33 (43) sts. Do not join.

ROW 1 (WS) *P1, k1; rep from * to last st, p1.

ROW 2 *K1, p1; rep from * to last st, k1.

SET-UP ROW (WS) P1, right lifted inc in next st, purl to end—34 (44) sts.

Work Rows 11–20 of Lace chart once, then rep Rows 1–20 until piece meas-

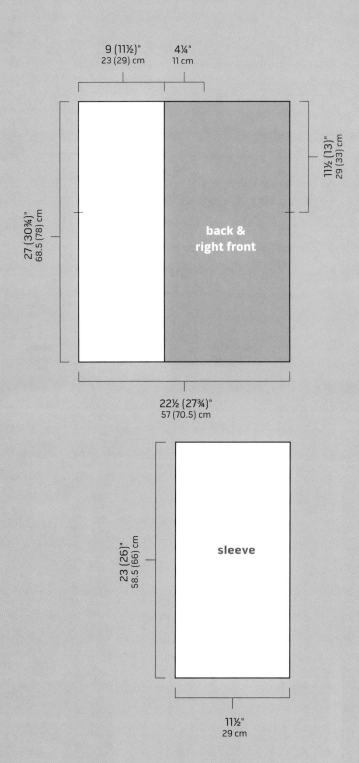

ures about 27 (30¾)" (68.5 [78] cm) from CO, ending with Row 10 of chart. Knit 2 rows—1 garter ridge on RS. Place all sts on holder.

Sleeves

With larger needle, CO 43 sts. Do not join. Purl 1 row. Rep Rows 1–8 of Sleeve chart until piece measures 23 (26)" (58.5 [66] cm) from CO, ending with Row 4 or 8 of chart. BO all sts.

Border

With smaller needle and RS facing, pick up and knit 96 (108) sts evenly spaced along one selvedge edge of sleeve. Do not join. Knit 6 rows. With WS facing, BO all sts very loosely—4 garter ridges on RS. Rep for other selvedge edge of sleeve.

Finishing

Join Shoulders

Place 84 (104) back sts onto one needle and 34 (44) right front sts onto a second needle. With RS tog and larger needle, use the three-needle method (see Glossary) to BO 34 (44) right front and back sts tog for right shoulder, then BO next 16 sts for back neck, then place 34 (44) left front sts onto second needle and BO 34 (44) left front sts tog with rem back sts for left shoulder. Press garment body and sleeves with warm iron to flatten knitted fabric.

Neckband

With smaller needle and RS facing, pick up and knit 97 (110) sts (about 2 sts for every 3 rows) along right front edge, 19 sts across back neck, and 97 (110) sts along left front edge—213 (239) sts total. Do not join.

SET-UP ROW Sl 1 pwise with yarn in front (wyf), knit to end.

Rep this row until piece measures 2" (5 cm) from pick-up row, ending with a WS row. Work 2 rows of single rib as foll:

ROW 1 Sl 1 pwise with yarn in back (wyb), *p1, k1; rep from * to end.

ROW 2 Sl 1 pwise wyf, *k1, p1; rep from * to end.

BO all sts loosely in patt.

Seams

With yarn threaded on a tapestry needle, join CO edge to BO edge of sleeve, using invisible horizontal grafting (see Glossary) for lace section and mattress st with 1-st seam allowance (see Glossary) for garter st. Press each seam flat. Pin sleeve to front and back, aligning center sleeve top to shoulder seam. With yarn threaded on a tapestry needle, sew sleeve in place, using a mattress st with ½-st seam allowance (see Glossary) for lace section on body and catching 1 strand of the BO edge on sleeve. Sew side seams up to lower edge of sleeve using a mattress st with ½-st seam allowance. Press seams flat with warm iron.

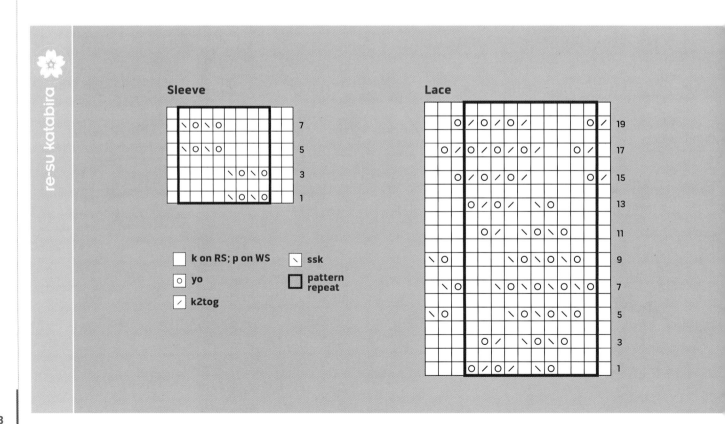

Sleeve

Lace

k on RS; p on WS

o yo

∕ k2tog

∖ ssk

pattern repeat

 # asian asymmetry

FINISHED SIZE

About 36 (40, 44)" (91.5 [101.5, 112] cm) chest circumference and 19½ (21, 22½)" (49.5 [53.5, 57] cm) in length. Top shown measures 36" (91.5 cm).

YARN

DK weight (#3 Light).

Shown here: Filatura di Crosa Brilla (42% cotton, 58% viscose rayon; 120 yd [110 m]/50 g): #393 royal blue, 8 (10, 11) balls.

NEEDLES

Size U.S. 4 (3.5 mm): 24" (60 cm) circular (cir) and extra needle the same size or smaller for three-needle bind-off.

Adjust needle size if necessary to obtain the correct gauge.

NOTIONS

Markers (m); stitch holders; size E/4 (3.5 mm) crochet hook; tapestry needle.

GAUGE

23 stitches and 30 rows = 4" (10 cm) in stockinette stitch.

Blue is a Japanese fashion color appropriate for late summer through winter. From sky blue to slate to deep navy, blue can be cool and serene or vivid and electric, as is the cobalt I used here.

Short sleeves, a stand-up collar, and an asymmetrical closure are all Asian design hallmarks, although perhaps not specifically Japanese. With a slight flare from bust to hip for a flattering fit, the twisted rib at the lower edge, neckband, and center sleeve is all the stitch texture that's needed. The yarn takes care of the rest of the visual appeal through a combination of matte and glossy twisted cotton that produces a subtle sheen similar to that found in one-color brocade weaves. The faux asymmetrical opening is, in fact, a V-neck—the neckband is sewn onto the front of the garment by hand.

This top is a strong statement individually and looks fabulous paired with the Nishiki kimono (page 56), where the blue really comes alive.

Back

CO 115 (127, 139) sts. Do not join.

ROW 1 (WS) *P1 through back loop (p1tbl), k1 through back loop (k1tbl); rep from * to last st, p1tbl.

ROW 2 *K1tbl, p1tbl; rep from * to last st, k1tbl.

Rep rows 1 and 2 until piece measures ¾" (2 cm) from CO, ending with a WS row. Change to St st (knit RS rows; purl WS rows) and work even until piece measures 2" (5 cm) from CO, ending with a WS row.

DEC ROW K1, ssk, knit to last 3 sts, k2tog, k1—2 sts dec'd.

Work even in St st for 13 rows. Rep the last 14 rows 5 more times—103 (115, 127) sts rem. Work even until piece measures 12 (13, 14)" (30.5 [33, 35.5] cm) from CO, ending with a WS row.

Shape Armholes

BO 4 sts at beg of next 2 rows, then BO 2 sts at beg of foll 2 rows—91 (103, 115) sts rem. Dec 1 st each end of needle every RS row 4 (6, 7) times—83 (91, 101) sts rem. Work even until armholes measure 7½ (8, 8½)" (19 [20.5, 21.5] cm), ending with a WS row. Place sts on holder.

Front

CO and work as for back until armholes measure 1¾ (2, 2¼)" (4.5 [5, 5.5] cm), ending with a RS row—83 (91, 101) sts.

DIVIDING ROW (WS) P41 (45, 50) and place these 41 (45, 50) sts on holder to work later for right neck, p2tog, p40 (44, 49)—41 (45, 50) sts rem for left neck.

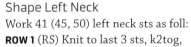

3½ (4, 4½)" 7½ (7¾, 8½)"
9 (10, 11.5) cm 19 (19.5, 21.5) cm

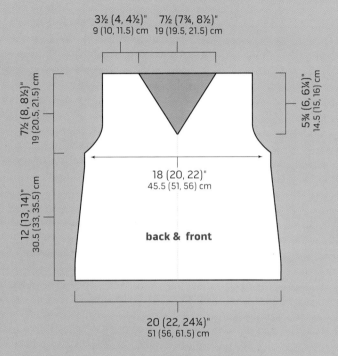

7½ (8, 8½)"
19 (20.5, 21.5) cm

5¾ (6, 6¼)"
14.5 (15, 16) cm

18 (20, 22)"
45.5 (51, 56) cm

12 (13, 14)"
30.5 (33, 35.5) cm

back & front

20 (22, 24¼)"
51 (56, 61.5) cm

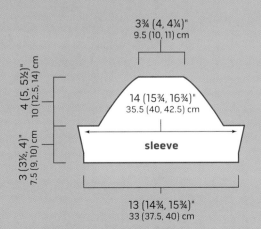

3¾ (4, 4¼)"
9.5 (10, 11) cm

4 (5, 5½)"
10 (12.5, 14) cm

14 (15¾, 16¾)"
35.5 (40, 42.5) cm

3 (3½, 4)"
7.5 (9, 10) cm

sleeve

13 (14¾, 15¾)"
33 (37.5, 40) cm

Shape Left Neck

Work 41 (45, 50) left neck sts as foll:

ROW 1 (RS) Knit to last 3 sts, k2tog, k1—1 st dec'd.

ROW 2 Purl.

Rep these 2 rows 20 (21, 23) more times—20 (23, 26) sts rem. Work even until armhole measures same as back. Place sts on holder.

Shape Right Neck

Transfer 41 (45, 50) held sts onto needle and join yarn at center front edge.

ROW 1 (RS) K1, ssk, knit to end—1 st dec'd.

ROW 2 Purl.

Rep these 2 rows 20 (21, 23) more times—20 (23, 26) sts rem. Work even until armhole measures same as back. Place sts on holder.

Sleeves

CO 75 (85, 91) sts. Do not join.

ROW 1 (WS) *P1tbl, k1tbl; rep from * to last st, p1tbl.

ROW 2 *K1tbl, p1tbl; rep from * to last st, k1tbl.

Rep Rows 1 and 2 until piece measures ¾" (2 cm) from CO, ending with a WS row.

INC ROW (RS) K1f&b, k31 (36, 39), place marker (pm), k1tbl, [p1tbl, k1tbl] 5 times, pm, knit to last 2 sts, k1f&b, k1—77 (87, 93) sts.

NEXT ROW (WS) Purl to m, slip marker (sl m), p1tbl, [k1tbl, p1tbl] 5 times, sl m, purl to end.

Work even, keeping the center 11 sts in twisted rib as established until piece measures 1½" (3.8 cm) from CO, ending with a WS row.

INC ROW (RS) K1f&b, work in patt to last 2 sts, k1f&b, k1—2 sts inc'd.
Work even until piece measures 2½" (6.5 cm) from CO, ending with a WS row, then work inc row once more—81 (91, 97) sts. Work even until piece measures 3 (3½, 4)" (7.5 [9, 10] cm) from CO, ending with a WS row.

Shape Cap

NOTE *Stitch pattern changes at the same time as the cap is shaped; read all the way through the foll section before proceeding.*
BO 4 sts at beg of next 2 rows, then BO 2 sts at beg of next 6 rows—61 (71, 77) sts rem. Dec 1 st each end of needle every RS row 7 (11, 13) times—47 (49, 51) sts rem. BO 2 sts at beg of next 2 rows, then BO 3 sts at beg of foll 4 rows—31 (33, 35) sts rem. BO 5 sts at beg of foll 2 rows—21 (23, 25) sts rem. BO all sts.

At the same time when piece measures 4 (4½, 5)" (10 [11.5, 12.5] cm) from CO, ending with a WS row, work as foll:
ROW 1 (RS) Knit to m, remove m, k2, pm, work 7 sts in twisted rib as established, pm, k2, remove m, knit to end.
ROW 2 Purl to m, sl m, work 7 sts in twisted rib as established, sl m, purl to end.
Work center twisted rib patt until piece measures 5 (5½, 6)" (12.5 [14, 15] cm) from CO. Discontinue twisted rib and work in St st to end of sleeve cap.

Neckband

CO 18 sts.
ROW 1 (WS) K1, [p1tbl, k1tbl] 8 times, p1.
ROW 2 (RS) Sl 1 kwise with yarn in back (wyb), [p1tbl, k1tbl] 8 times, p1.
Rep these 2 rows until piece measures 28 (30, 33)" (71 [76, 84] cm) from CO. Leave sts on needle until most of the neckband has been sewn on to ensure the band is the correct length.

Finishing

Join Shoulders

Place 83 (91, 101) held back sts onto one needle and 20 (23, 26) held right front sts onto another needle. With RS tog, use the three-needle method (see Glossary) to BO 20 (23, 26) right front and 20 (23, 26) back sts tog for right shoulder, then BO the next 43 (45, 49) back sts as usual, then place 20 (23, 26) held left front sts onto second needle and BO 20 (23, 26) left front sts tog with rem 20 (23, 26) back sts for left shoulder.

Seams

With yarn threaded on a tapestry needle, use a mattress st with ½-st seam allowance (see Glossary) to sew side and sleeve seams. With a crochet hook, use slip st crochet (see Glossary) to join sleeve cap to armhole, matching side and sleeve seams and matching center sleeve cap to shoulder seam, easing in fullness at cap as necessary and working from the body (not the sleeve) side of the join.

Neckband

Turn garment RS out and pin the non-slipped st selvedge edge of the neckband to neck opening, beg at the right front V, working across the back neck, and ending at the left front V, stretching slightly to eliminate ripples. Angle the remaining neckband across the body to just under the right armhole. Knit or re-move extra rows as necessary to achieve correct length. BO all sts in patt. With yarn threaded on a tapestry needle, use a mattress st with ½-st seam allowance from the neckline and capturing the purl bump on the edge of the neckband to sew band in place around the neck opening. Use a running st (see Glossary) to secure the neckband onto the right front of the garment across the body to the armhole, stitching the BO end of the band in line with the side seam.

Lightly steam-block seams.

suo amanuno

FINISHED SIZE

About 36 (39, 42, 45, 48)" (91.5
[99, 106.5, 114.5, 122] cm) in circumference and 20½ (21, 22, 23½,
24)" (52 [53.5, 56, 59.5, 61] cm) in
length. Top shown measures 36"
(91.5 cm).

YARN

Sportweight (#2 Fine).

Shown here: Louet Euroflax
Sport (100% wet-spun linen;
270 yd [247 m]/100 g): #42 eggplant, 3 (3, 3, 4, 4) skeins.

NEEDLES

Size U.S. 8 (5 mm): 24" (60 cm)
circular (cir); size U.S. 6 (4 mm):
24" (60 cm) cir; size U.S. 4
(3.5 mm): 24" (60 cm) cir; size
U.S. 3 (3.25 mm): 16" (40 cm) cir.

*Adjust needle size if necessary
to obtain the correct gauge.*

NOTIONS

Stitch holders; marker (m); size
C/2 (2.75 mm) crochet hook;
tapestry needle.

GAUGE

21 stitches and 30 rows = 4"
(10 cm) in stockinette stitch on
second-to-smallest needle.

Suo, or maroon, falls in the range of warm reds. It is a deep, rich saturated blend of brown, red, and purple. Suo is the name of the sappanwood tree from which the dye comes. *Amanuno* is linen—a bast fiber of ancient heritage. The graceful drape of linen is amplified as it is pressed, worn, washed, and handled.

This top's semi-fitted waistline flares to a basketweave pattern at the lower edge. A simple garter ridge finishes the armhole and jewel neck edges. In its simplicity, this piece is elegant by itself, but also layers well under many kimono, such as the Re-Su Katabira (page 64), Nishiki kimono (page 56), and Shimofuri Chairo Ke-Bura (page 20). Suo Amanuno will translate well into any color—it is a classy wardrobe basic that's better than the T-shirt!

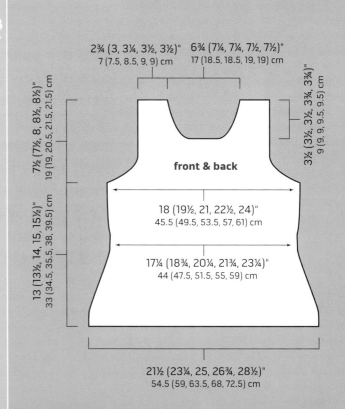

suo amanuno

2¾ (3, 3¼, 3½, 3½)"
7 (7.5, 8.5, 9, 9) cm

6¾ (7¼, 7¼, 7½, 7½)"
17 (18.5, 18.5, 19, 19) cm

3½ (3½, 3½, 3¾, 3¾)"
9 (9, 9, 9.5, 9.5) cm

7½ (7½, 8, 8½, 8½)"
19 (19, 20.5, 21.5, 21.5) cm

13 (13½, 14, 15, 15½)"
33 (34.5, 35.5, 38, 39.5) cm

front & back

18 (19½, 21, 22½, 24)"
45.5 (49.5, 53.5, 57, 61) cm

17¼ (18¾, 20¼, 21¾, 23¼)"
44 (47.5, 51.5, 55, 59) cm

21½ (23¼, 25, 26¾, 28½)"
54.5 (59, 63.5, 68, 72.5) cm

Back

With largest needle, CO 98 (106, 114, 122, 130) sts. Do not join.

ROW 1 (RS) K1, [k4, p4] 12 (13, 14, 15, 16) times, k1.

ROW 2 P1, [k4, p4] 12 (13, 14, 15, 16) times, p1.

Rep Rows 1 and 2 three more times, then work Row 1 once more. Change to second-to-largest needle and work Row 2 once more—10 rows total. Shift patt as foll:

ROW 1 (RS) K1, [p4, k4] 12 (13, 14, 15, 16) times, k1.

ROW 2 P1, [p4, k4] 12 (13, 14, 15, 16) times, p1.

Rep these 2 rows once more, then work Row 1 once again. Change to second-to-smallest needle and work Row 2 once more—16 rows total from CO. Work 6 rows even in St st (knit RS rows; purl WS rows).

DEC ROW (RS) K2, k2tog, knit to last 4 sts, ssk, k2—2 sts dec'd.

Work 5 rows even in St st. Rep the last 6 rows 3 more times—90 (98, 106, 114, 122) sts rem. Work even until piece measures 8 (8½, 8½, 9, 9½)" (20.5 [21.5, 21.5, 23, 24] cm) from CO, ending with a WS row.

INC ROW (RS) K2, M1 (see Glossary), knit to last 2 sts, M1, k2—2 sts inc'd.

Work even until piece measures 10 (10½, 11, 11½, 12)" (25.5 [26.5, 28, 29, 30.5] cm) from CO, ending with a WS row. Rep inc row—94 (102, 110, 118, 126) sts. Work even until piece measures 13 (13½, 14, 15, 15½)" (33 [34.5, 35.5, 38, 39.5] cm) from CO, ending with a WS row.

Shape Armholes

BO 5 sts at beg of next 2 rows, then BO 3 sts at beg of next 2 rows, then BO 2 sts at beg of foll 2 rows—74 (82, 90, 98, 106) sts rem.

DEC ROW (RS) K1, k2tog, knit to last 3 sts, ssk, k1—2 sts dec'd.

Rep dec row every RS row 3 (5, 8, 10, 13) more times—66 (70, 72, 76, 78) sts rem. Work even until armholes measure 4 (4, 4½, 4¾, 4¾)" (10 [10, 11.5, 12, 12] cm), ending with a WS row.

Shape Neck

(RS) K26 (27, 28, 29, 30) for right shoulder, join new yarn and BO center 14 (16, 16, 18, 18) sts for back neck, knit to end for left shoulder—26 (27, 28, 29, 30) sts rem each side. Working each side separately, at each neck edge BO 3 sts once, then BO 2 sts 2 times—19 (20, 21, 22, 23) sts rem each side. Dec 1 st at each neck edge every RS row 4 times—15 (16, 17, 18, 19) sts rem. Work even until armholes measure 7½ (7½, 8, 8½, 8½)" (19 [19, 20.5, 21.5, 21.5] cm), ending with a WS row. Place sts on holders.

Front

Work the same as for the back.

Finishing

Join Shoulders

Place 15 (16, 17, 18, 19) held left back shoulder sts onto one needle and 15 (16, 17, 18, 19) held left front shoulder sts onto a second needle. With RS tog and second-to-smallest needle, use the three-needle method (see Glossary) to BO the sts tog. Cut yarn and draw tail through last st to secure. Rep for right shoulder.

Seams

With yarn threaded on a tapestry needle and RS facing, use the mattress st with 1-st seam allowance (see Glossary) to sew side seams.

Armbands

With smallest cir needle, RS facing, and beg at base of armhole, pick up and knit 47 (47, 50, 53, 53) sts along front armhole and 47 (47, 50, 53, 53) sts along back armhole—94 (94, 100, 106, 106) sts total. Place marker (pm) and join for working in rnds. Purl 1 rnd, then knit 1 rnd. BO all sts pwise.

Neckband

With smallest cir needle and RS facing, pick up and knit 60 (64, 64, 66, 66) sts across front neck and 60 (64, 64, 66, 66) sts across back neck—120 (128, 128, 132, 132) sts total. Pm and join for working in rnds. Purl 1 rnd, then knit 1 rnd. BO all sts pwise.

Press garment with iron set for linen.

# keshi murasaki

FINISHED SIZE

About 36½ (41, 45½)" (92.5 [104, 115.5] cm) in circumference and 21½ (22½, 23½)" (54.5 [57, 59.5] cm) in length to side, plus 2½" (6.5 cm) to center front. Top shown measures 36½" (92.5 cm).

YARN

Sportweight (#2 Fine).

Shown here: Lana Grossa Cambio (70% cotton, 30% nylon; 137 yd [125 m]/50 g): #018 gray-purple, 6 (7, 8) skeins.

NEEDLES

Size U.S. 5 (3.75 mm): 24" (60 cm) circular (cir) plus extra needle same size or smaller for three-needle bind-off.

Adjust needle size if necessary to obtain the correct gauge.

NOTIONS

Stitch holders; removable markers; size F/5 (3.75 mm) crochet hook; tapestry needle.

GAUGE

24 stitches and 36 rows = 4" (10 cm) in seed stitch.

Keshi murasaki, a grayed mauve, is one of the wide range of purples dyed from gromwell root. I used a microfiber-wrapped cotton yarn to give a luminescent sheen to the seed-stitch texture of this simple shell. Geometric stair steps along the lower edge and neckline call to mind the small geometric patterning in woven solid-color Japanese textiles.

The top can stand alone, but is beautifully paired with the Mijikui Dofuku (page 86), a short kimono that barely skims the waist to highlight the geometric detail of the seed-stitch top.

stitch guide

**SEED STITCH
(odd number of sts)**

ALL ROWS *K1, p1; rep from * to last st, k1.

Back

CO 23 (27, 31) sts. Do not join. Work in seed st (see Stitch Guide) for 5 rows, ending with a WS row. Shape lower edge as foll: With RS facing, use the cable method (see Glossary) to CO 10 (11, 12) sts at beg of needle, then, beg with newly CO sts, work in seed st to end—10 (11, 12) sts inc'd. With WS facing, use the cable method to CO 10 (11, 12) sts at beg of needle, then beg with newly CO sts, work in seed st to end—10 (11, 12) sts inc'd. Work 2 rows even in patt. Rep the last 4 rows 3 more times—103 (115, 127) sts. Use the cable method to CO 6 (7, 8) sts at the beg of the next 2 rows in the same manner—115 (129, 143) sts. Work even in seed st for 6 rows—piece measures about ¾" (2 cm) from last CO row.

Shape Waist

DEC ROW (RS) Work p2tog or k2tog as necessary to maintain patt, work in seed st to last 2 sts, work p2tog or k2tog as necessary to maintain patt—2 sts dec'd.

Work even in seed st for 7 rows. Rep the last 8 rows 2 more times—109 (123, 137) sts rem. Work even until piece measures 14 (14½, 15)" (35.5 [37, 38] cm) from last cable CO at side edge, ending with a WS row.

Shape Armholes

Keeping in patt, BO 5 sts at beg of next 2 rows, then BO 3 sts at beg of next 2 rows, then BO 2 sts at beg of foll 2 rows—89 (103, 117) sts rem. Dec 1 st at each end of needle every RS row 2 (6, 10) times—85 (91, 97) sts rem. Work even in patt until armholes measure 7 (7½, 8)" (18 [19, 20.5] cm), ending with a WS row.

Shape Neck

(RS) Keeping in patt, work 24 (26, 28) sts for right shoulder, join new yarn and BO 37 (39, 41) sts for back neck, work to end—24 (26, 28) sts rem at each side. Working each side separately, work even for 5 rows. Place sts on holders.

Front

CO and work as for back until armholes measure 1 (1½, 2)" (2.5 [3.8, 5] cm), ending with a WS row. Cont armhole shaping if necessary and *at the same time* shape neck as foll.

Shape Neck

Mark center 9 (11, 13) sts. With RS facing and keeping in patt, work to m, then place these sts on holder for left

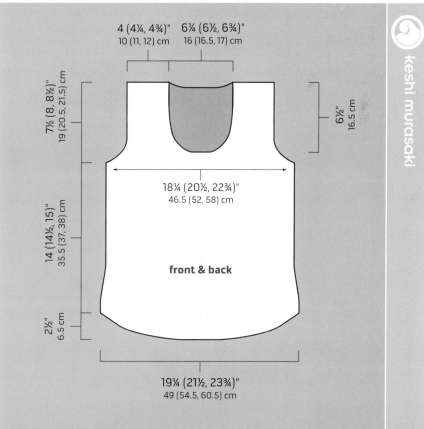

4 (4¼, 4¾)"
10 (11, 12) cm

6¼ (6½, 6¾)"
16 (16.5, 17) cm

7½ (8, 8½)"
19 (20.5, 21.5) cm

6½"
16.5 cm

18¼ (20½, 22¾)"
46.5 (52, 58) cm

14 (14½, 15)"
35.5 (37, 38) cm

front & back

2½"
6.5 cm

19¼ (21½, 23¾)"
49 (54.5, 60.5) cm

keshi murasaki

83

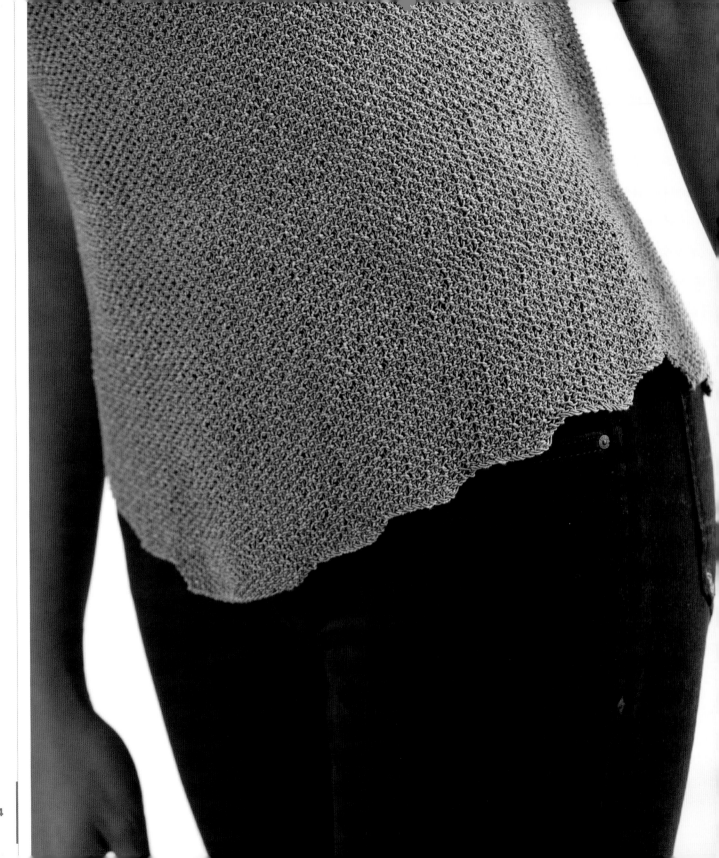

shoulder, BO marked 9 (11, 13) sts, work to end for right shoulder.

Right Neck

Keeping in patt, work 3 rows even.
NEXT ROW (RS) BO 7 sts, work to end—7 sts dec'd.
Work 3 rows even. Rep the last 4 rows once more—24 (26, 28) sts rem when all neck and armhole shaping is complete. Work even until armhole measures 7½ (8, 8½)" (19 [20.5, 21.5] cm), ending with a WS row. Place sts on holder and cut yarn, leaving a 24" (61 cm) tail for seaming.

Left Neck

Return held left neck sts onto needle and join yarn at neck edge with WS facing. Keeping in patt, work 4 rows even.
NEXT ROW (WS) BO 7 sts, work to end—7 sts dec'd.
Work 3 rows even. Rep the last 4 rows once more—24 (26, 28) sts rem when all neck and armhole shaping is complete. Work even until armhole measures 7½ (8, 8½)" (19 [20.5, 21.5] cm), ending with a WS row. Place sts on holder and cut yarn, leaving a 24" (61 cm) tail for seaming.

Join Shoulders

Place 24 (26, 28) left back shoulder sts onto one needle and 24 (26, 28) left front shoulder sts onto second needle. With RS tog, use tail and three-needle method (see Glossary) to BO the sts tog. Pull tail through rem st to secure. Rep for right shoulder.

Finishing

Wet-block (see Glossary) garment to measurements, pinning each geometric stair-step at lower edge and neckline. Let air-dry completely.

Seams

With yarn threaded on a tapestry needle, use the mattress st (see Glossary), capturing purl bars of seed st, to sew side seams.

Armbands

With crochet hook and beg and end at base of armhole, work 1 row of single crochet (sc; see Glossary) around armhole—about 80 (86, 90) sc.

Weave in loose ends. Lightly steam seams to set sts.

mijikui dofuku

FINISHED SIZE

About 40½ (45, 49½)" (103 [114.5, 125.5] cm) in circumference and 18 (19, 20)" (45.5 [48.5, 51] cm) in length. Kimono shown measures 40½" (103 cm).

YARN

Sportweight (#2 Fine).

Shown here: Lana Grossa Cambio (70% cotton, 30% nylon; 137 yd [125 m]/50 g): #018 gray-purple (A), 8 (9, 10) skeins; #10 green (B), 2 skeins.

NEEDLES

Body and Sleeves: size U.S. 4 (3.5 mm): 24" (60 cm) circular (cir). *Edging:* size U.S. 3 (3.25 mm): 24" (60 cm) cir.

Adjust needle size if necessary to obtain the correct gauge.

NOTIONS

Stitch holders; removable markers; tapestry needle.

GAUGE

23 stitches and 32 rows = 4" (10 cm) in stockinette stitch on larger needle.

Dofuku is a short battle-jacket style that I have made even shorter in this design, making it perfect for layering over the Keshi Murasaki (page 80), a coordinating top of the same keshi murasaki color. According to one Japanese traditional calendar, grayed mauve paired with burgundy is an early autumn/September color scheme. Pair it with deep blue for a winter/ December combination. This pair takes the sweater set into a new dimension of elegance.

The smooth stockinette stitch in this design is interrupted only by a narrow reverse stockinette-stitch roll at the front neck and sleeve cuff, where the subtle color change is just enough to enhance the main color.

Back

With A and smaller needle, CO 117 (129, 143) sts. Do not join.

ROW 1 (WS) P1, *k1 through back loop (k1tbl), p1 through back loop (p1tbl); rep from * to last 2 sts, k1tbl, p1.

ROW 2 K1, *p1tbl, k1tbl; rep from * to last 2 sts, p1tbl, k1.

Rep these 2 rows once more, then work Row 1 once again—5 rows total. Change to St st and knit 1 row. Change to larger needle and work even in St st until piece measures 18 (19, 20)" (45.5 [48.5, 51] cm) from CO, ending with a WS row. Place sts on holder.

Right Front

With A and smaller needle, CO 67 (75, 81) sts. Do not join.

ROW 1 (WS) P1, *k1tbl, p1tbl; rep from * to last 2 sts, k1tbl, p1.

ROW 2 K1, *p1tbl, k1tbl; rep from * to last 2 sts, p1tbl, k1.

Rep these 2 rows once more, then work Row 1 once again—5 rows total. Change to St st and knit 1 row. Change to larger needle and work even in St st until piece measures 5" (12.5 cm) from CO, ending with a WS row.

Shape Neck

DEC ROW (RS) BO 2 sts, knit to end— 2 sts dec'd.

Purl 1 (WS) row. Rep the last 2 rows 3 more times—59 (67, 73) sts rem.

DEC ROW (RS) K1, ssk, knit to end— 1 st dec'd.

Purl 1 (WS) row. Rep the last 2 rows 4 (6, 8) more times—54 (60, 64) sts rem.

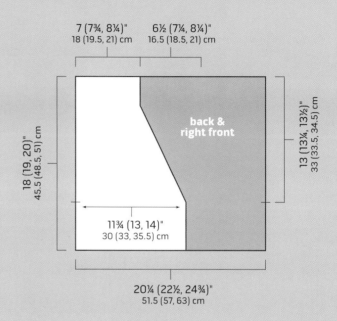

7 (7¾, 8¼)"
18 (19.5, 21) cm

6½ (7¼, 8¼)"
16.5 (18.5, 21) cm

back & right front

13 (13¼, 13½)"
33 (33.5, 34.5) cm

18 (19, 20)"
45.5 (48.5, 51) cm

11¾ (13, 14)"
30 (33, 35.5) cm

20¼ (22½, 24¾)"
51.5 (57, 63) cm

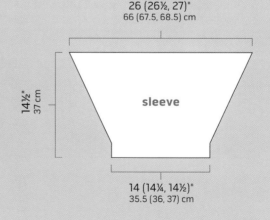

26 (26½, 27)"
66 (67.5, 68.5) cm

sleeve

14½"
37 cm

14 (14¼, 14½)"
35.5 (36, 37) cm

Rep dec row every 4th row 10 (12, 12) times, then every 6th row 4 times—40 (44, 48) sts rem. Work even until piece measures 18 (19, 20)" (45.5 [48.5, 51] cm) from CO, ending with a WS row. Place sts on holder.

Left Front

With A and smaller needle, CO 67 (75, 81) sts. Do not join.

ROW 1 (WS) P1, *k1tbl, p1tbl; rep from * to last 2 sts, k1tbl, p1.

ROW 2 K1, *p1tbl, k1tbl; rep from * to last 2 sts, p1tbl, k1.

Rep these 2 rows once more, then work Row 1 once again—5 rows total. Change to St st and knit 1 row. Change to larger needle and work even in St st until piece measures 5" (12.5 cm) from CO, ending with a RS row.

Shape Neck

DEC ROW (WS) BO 2 sts, purl to end—2 sts dec'd.

Knit 1 (RS) row. Rep the last 2 rows 3 more times—59 (67, 73) sts rem. Purl 1 (WS) row.

DEC ROW (RS) Knit to last 3 sts, k2tog, k1—1 st dec'd.

Purl 1 (WS) row. Rep the last 2 rows 4 (6, 8) more times—54 (60, 64) sts rem. Rep dec row every 4th row 10 (12, 12) times, then every 6th row 4 times—40 (44, 48) sts rem. Work even until piece measures 18 (19, 20)" (45.5 [48.5, 51] cm) from CO, ending with a WS row. Place sts on holder.

Join Shoulders

Place 117 (129, 143) held back sts onto

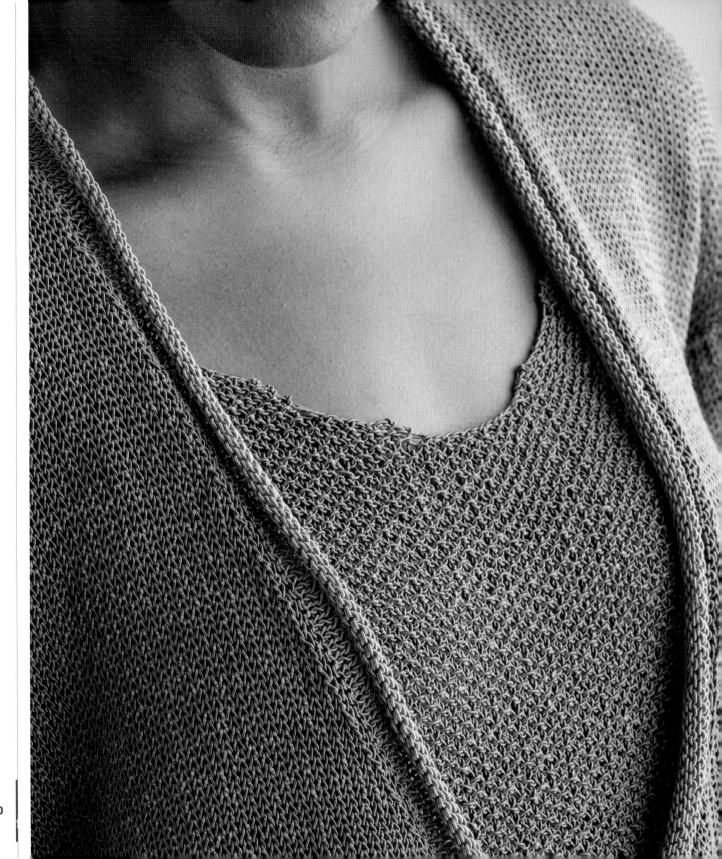

one needle and 40 (44, 48) held right front sts onto another needle. With A, larger needle, and RS tog, use the three-needle method (see Glossary) to BO 40 (44, 48) right front and 40 (44, 48) back sts tog for right shoulder, then BO the next 37 (41, 47) back sts as usual, then place 40 (44, 48) held left front sts onto second needle and BO 40 (44, 48) left front sts tog with rem 40 (44, 48) back sts for left shoulder.

Sleeves

Measure and mark front and back 13 (13¼, 13½)" (33 [33.5, 34.5] cm) down from shoulder for sleeve placement. With A, larger needle, and RS facing, pick up and knit 148 (150, 152) sts evenly spaced between markers. Knit 1 (WS) row for garter ridge. Dec 1 st at each end of needle on next row and every foll 3rd row 34 times as foll:

RS ROWS K1, ssk, knit to last 3 sts, k2tog, k1—2 sts dec'd.

WS ROWS P1, p2tog, purl to last 3 sts, ssp (see Glossary), p1—2 sts dec'd.

After all decs have been made (80 [82, 84] sts rem), work even until piece measures 13" (33 cm) from garter ridge, ending with a RS row. Change to smaller needle and knit 6 rows, ending with a RS row—3 garter ridges on RS.

Cuff

Change to B and purl 1 (WS) row. Change to larger needle and work even in St st until cuff measures 1" (2.5 cm) from last garter ridge, ending with a WS row. BO all sts. Cuff will naturally roll to reveal purl side.

Finishing

Wet-block to measurements. Let air-dry completely. With A threaded on a tapestry needle and using the mattress st with ½-st seam allowance for lower rib and 1-st seam allowance (see Glossary) for side and sleeves, sew sleeve and side seams except for sleeve cuff. With B threaded on a tapestry needle, WS facing, and using the mattress st for rev St st with 1-st seam allowance, sew cuff seam. With B, tack BO edge of cuff to first row of B to encourage St st roll.

Neckband

With A, smaller needle, RS facing, and beg at lower right front edge, pick up and knit 28 sts to corner at beg of neckline shaping, 2 sts close to the corner and place a removable marker in each st, 80 (86, 92) sts along right front curved neckline, 37 (41, 47) sts across back neck, 80 (86, 92) sts along left front curved neckline to corner at beg of neckline shaping, 2 sts close to the corner and place a removable marker in each st, and 28 sts along left front edge to lower edge—257 (273, 291) sts total. Knit 1 (WS) row to create a garter ridge on RS. Change to B and knit, working k1f&b (see Glossary) in each of the 4 marked sts—4 sts inc'd. Work in St st until piece measures 1" (2.5 cm) from garter ridge, ending with a WS row. BO all sts. With B threaded on a tapestry needle, tack lower front corners of BO edge to first row of B to encourage St st roll.

Weave in loose ends.

murasaki akai

FINISHED SIZE

About 49" (124.5 cm) in circumference—46½" (118 cm) garment plus a 2½" (6.5 cm) gap at center front—and 24" (61 cm) in length.

YARN

Worsted weight (#4 Medium).

Shown here: Brown Sheep Company Cotton Fleece (80% cotton, 20% wool; 215 yd [197 m]/100 g): #775 deep maroon (A), 5 skeins; #695 lilac haze (B), 3 skeins; #780 hearty merlot (C), #730 raging purple (D), and #935 salmon berry red (E), 1 skein each.

NEEDLES

Body and sleeves: size U.S. 7 (4.5 mm): two 24" (60 cm) circular (cir) and one double-pointed (dpn). *Bobbles:* size U.S. 6 (4 mm): set of 2 dpn.

Adjust needle size if necessary to obtain the correct gauge.

NOTIONS

Stitch holders; removable markers; size H/8 (5 mm) crochet hook; tapestry needle.

GAUGE

18 stitches and 36 rows (18 garter ridges) = 4" (10 cm) in garter stitch on larger needle; 20 stitches and 28 rows = 4" (10 cm) in reverse stockinette stitch on larger needle.

Purple and red is a royal color combination. For this kimono, I used a range of *murasaki* purples, from *usuki* (pale violet) to *fugi* (wisteria) to *ebi* (red violet) to *koki* (deep violet). The front and back panels feature garter-stitch short-rows that create triangles and rectangles in a bold graphic. The center back panel is attached to the side back panels as it is knitted. *Akai* (true red) bobbles are added at the end.

Light cotton unlined kimono are typically worn in the summer months; the matte cotton I used for this design is comfortable for all seasons. Colors for kimono, layering, and for surface decoration vary with the season and the month within the season. A traditional school of Japanese etiquette lists lavender and burgundy as the color scheme for September. This kimono not only fits with tradition, it is also contemporary in its presentation and wearability.

Back and Front Panels (make 4)

With E, larger needle, and using the long-tail method (see Glossary), CO 42 sts. Do not join. Knit 2 rows. Cut off E. Join C and D and work short-row (see Glossary) rectangle section as foll (first triangle plus second triangle makes one rectangle), carrying unused yarn along selvedge edge. Avoid pulling yarn too tightly.

First Triangle

With C, knit 2 rows.

SHORT-ROW 1 With D, k39, wrap next st, turn, knit to end.

SHORT-ROW 2 With C, k36, wrap next st, turn, knit to end.

SHORT-ROW 3 With D, k33, wrap next st, turn, knit to end.

Cont in this manner, alternating colors every 2 rows and knitting 3 fewer sts before turning on every short-row 9 more times.

NEXT SHORT-ROW With D, k3, wrap next st, turn, knit to end—first triangle complete. Cut off D.

Second Triangle

With C, knit 3 rows (do not hide wraps as you go), ending at the left selvedge edge. Cont in short-rows as foll:

SHORT-ROW 1 With D, p39, wrap next st, turn, purl to end.

SHORT-ROW 2 With C, p36, wrap next st, turn, purl to end.

Cont to alternate colors every 2 rows and purl 3 fewer sts before turning on every short-row 10 more times.

NEXT SHORT-ROW With D, p3, wrap next st, turn, purl to end.

Cut off D. Change to C and purl 3 rows (do not hide wraps as you go), ending at the right selvedge edge—second triangle and full rectangle complete. Cut off C.

Remaining Rectangles

Change to A and B, and beg with A, rep first triangle and second triangle 5 more times—6 rectangles complete. Place sts on holder.

Join Panels

Return 42 held sts of one panel to one cir needle and 42 held sts of a second panel to another cir needle. With A and WS tog, use the three-needle method

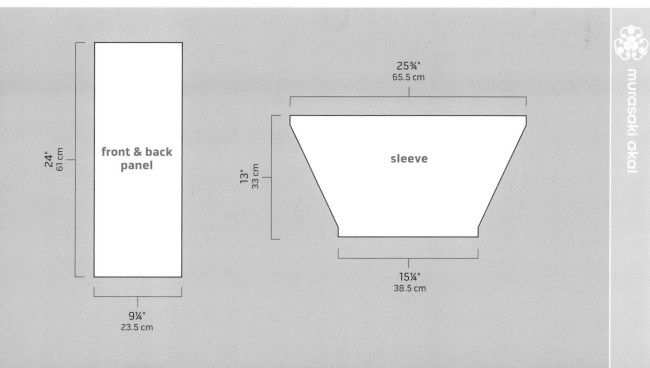

front & back panel

24"
61 cm

9¼"
23.5 cm

sleeve

25¾"
65.5 cm

13"
33 cm

15¼"
38.5 cm

(see Glossary) to BO the sts tog. Rep for rem two panels.

Wet-block (see Glossary) panels to measurements, squaring the corners to counteract the trapezoidal pull.

Sleeves

Measure and mark 13" (33 cm) down from shoulder on both front and back. With E, larger needle, RS facing, and beg at base of armhole, pick up and knit 116 sts evenly spaced between markers. Do not join. Knit 1 WS row. With C, knit 2 rows. With E, knit 2 rows. With C, knit 2 rows. With A, knit 2 rows, then purl 1 row, then knit 1 row—piece measures about 1" (2.5 cm) from pick-up row.

DEC ROW (RS) P1, p2tog, purl to last 3 sts, p2tog, p1—2 sts dec'd.

Work 3 rows even in rev St st (purl RS rows; knit WS rows). Rep the last 4 rows 19 more times, ending with a WS row—76 sts rem.

With RS facing, join C and knit 2 rows. With E, knit 2 rows. With C, knit 2 rows. With E, knit 1 row—piece measures about 13" (33 cm) from pick-up row. With WS facing, BO all sts kwise.

Center Back Borders

*With E, larger cir needle, and RS facing, pick up and knit 99 sts along center back edge of one panel. Knit 1 WS row. Join C and knit 2 rows. With E, knit 2 rows. With C, knit 2 rows. Set aside.

With second larger cir needle, rep from * for second center back edge.

Center Back Panel

Connect the center back panel to the live sts from each cir needle as you work from the lower hem to neck as foll:

With E and dpn, CO 20 sts. Turn work and hold in left hand. Place needle holding right back sts in your right hand. Sl 1 pwise with yarn in front (wyf) from right back needle to left needle, bring yarn to back, k2tog, k18, ssk (last center back st with first st of left back). Set dpn aside. Working back and forth on cir needles, turn, k20, turn. [*Sl 1 pwise wyf from right back needle to left needle, bring yarn to back, change to A and k2tog, k18, ssk, turn, k20, turn; rep from * once. **Sl 1 pwise wyf from right back needle to left needle, bring yarn to back, change to D and k2tog, k18, ssk, turn, k20, turn; rep from ** until there are 14 garter ridges in D] 6 times. Sl 1 pwise wyf from right back needle to left needle, bring yarn to back, change to E and cont to connect center back panel to right back with k2tog and connect center back panel to left back with ssk, work 3 rows with E—1 garter ridge in E. With E and WS facing, BO 20 rem sts.

Finishing

Weave in loose ends.

Neckband

With A, larger needle, RS facing, and beg at lower right center front, pick up and knit 100 sts evenly spaced along right front, 26 sts across back neck (1 st in each "ditch" of the vertical garter ridges and 1 st in each BO st), and 100 sts along left front, ending at lower edge of center left front—226 sts total. Work in garter st (knit every row) until band measures 1½" (3.8 cm) from pick-up row, ending with a WS row. Change to E and knit 1 row. With WS facing, BO all sts kwise. Wet-block to measurements. Let air-dry completely.

Bobbles (make 6)

Cut a strand of E about 36" (91.5 cm) long. Holding yarn on WS, insert a smaller dpn into center of color D square and draw a loop onto the needle. Leaving an 8" (20.5 cm) tail on the WS, use crochet hook to pull rem long end of strand through to RS in an adjacent space above st on needle. Using long end of strand as working yarn, work bobble as foll: (K1, yo, k1, yo, k1) in same st, turn, p5, turn, k5, then pass the second, third, fourth, and fifth sts over the first and off the needle. Pull the tail through the last st to secure. Thread tail on a tapestry needle, insert to WS, adjust position as necessary to center bobble, and tie ends into a square knot. Weave in loose ends.

Wet-block flat to measurements. Let air-dry completely.

Seams

With A threaded on a tapestry needle, use a mattress st for garter st (see Glossary) to sew side seams. Use a mattress st for rev St st (see Glossary) to sew sleeve seams, changing to garter st at cuff and sleeve top. Lightly steam seams to set sts.

re-su yukata

FINISHED SIZE
About 50" (127 cm) in circumference and 48" (122 cm) in length.

YARN
Chunky weight (#5 Bulky).

Shown here: Crystal Palace Cotton Chenille (100% cotton; 98 yd [90 m]/50 g): #2230 mango, 17 balls.

NEEDLES
Body: size U.S. 9 (5.5 mm): 24" (60 cm) circular (cir).
Sleeves and Edging: size U.S. 7 (4.5 mm): 24" (60 cm) cir and set of 2 double-pointed (dpn).

Adjust needle size if necessary to obtain the correct gauge.

NOTIONS
Stitch holders or waste yarn; tapestry needle; size H/8 (5 mm) crochet hook; one 2" x 1¼" (5 x 3.2 cm) button; about 24" (61 cm) of cotton yarn to attach button.

GAUGE
13 stitches and 18 rows = 4" (10 cm) in arrowhead lace pattern on larger needle; 12 stitches and 22 rows = 4" (10 cm) in stockinette stitch on smaller needle.

A mixture of *kurenai* (scarlet pink) and *ki* (pure yellow), this clear, warm mango color fits the Japanese color palette for late spring and summer. *Yukata* is a bathrobe or a casual kimono to wear at home. The velvety soft texture of cotton chenille worked in an easy chevron lace pattern makes an exquisite full-length kimono that will find its way out the door to a special event.

I designed this piece with a square neckline that is closed with an unusual ceramic button and a simple knitted cord button loop. The garter-stitch neckband is an adventure, with some of the band attached to the garment as it is knitted and some seamed onto the garment afterward (to measure accurately, count the garter ridges). Stockinette-stitch sleeves with garter-stitch cuffs are a visual relief from all the texture and detail.

stitch guide

ARROWHEAD LACE
(multiple of 10 sts + 1)

ROW 1 (RS) K1, *[yo, sl 1, k1, psso] 2 times, k1, [k2tog, yo] 2 times, k1; rep from *.

ROW 2 Purl.

ROW 3 K1, *k1, yo, sl 1, k1, psso, yo, sl 1, k2tog, psso, yo, k2tog, yo, k2; rep from *.

ROW 4 Purl.

Repeat Rows 1–4 for pattern.

Back

With larger needle, CO 81 sts. Do not join. Purl 1 row. Rep Rows 1–4 of arrowhead lace patt (see Stitch Guide) until piece measures 38" (96.5 cm) from CO, ending with a WS row.

Shape Armholes
BO 10 sts at beg of next 2 rows—61 sts rem. Cont in patt as established until armholes measure 10" (25.5 cm), ending with a WS row. Place sts on waste yarn holder.

Front (make 2)

With larger needle, CO 41 sts. Do not join. Purl 1 row. Rep Rows 1–4 of arrowhead lace patt until piece measures 38" (96.5 cm) from CO, ending with a WS row. (Count the lace reps at the side edge to ensure the front has the same number of rows as the back to the armhole.)

Shape Armhole and Neck
BO 10 sts at beg of next 2 rows—21 sts rem. Cont in patt as established until armhole measures 10" (25.5 cm), ending with a WS row. Place sts on waste yarn holder.

Sleeves

With smaller needle, CO 40 sts. Do not join. Work in garter st (knit every row) until piece measures 2" (5 cm) from CO, ending with a WS row. Change to St st (knit RS rows; purl WS rows) and work even until piece measures 4" (10 cm) from CO, ending with a WS row.
INC ROW K1, right lifted inc (RLI; see Glossary) into next st, knit to last st, left lifted inc (LLI; see Glossary), k1—2 sts inc'd.

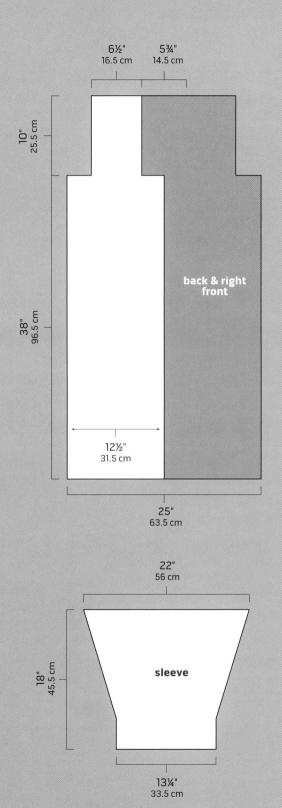

6½"
16.5 cm

5¾"
14.5 cm

10"
25.5 cm

back & right
front

38"
96.5 cm

12½"
31.5 cm

25"
63.5 cm

22"
56 cm

18"
45.5 cm

sleeve

13¼"
33.5 cm

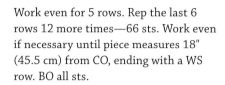
Work even for 5 rows. Rep the last 6 rows 12 more times—66 sts. Work even if necessary until piece measures 18" (45.5 cm) from CO, ending with a WS row. BO all sts.

Finishing

Wet-block (see Glossary) all pieces to measurements. Let air-dry completely.

Join Shoulders

Place 61 held back sts onto one needle and 21 held right front sts onto a second needle. With RS tog and larger needle, use the three-needle method (see Glossary) to BO 21 right front sts tog with 21 back sts for right shoulder, BO next 19 back sts for back neck, then place 21 held left front sts onto a second needle and use the three-needle method to BO 21 left front sts to rem 21 back sts for left shoulder. Cut yarn and pull tail through rem st to secure. Lightly steam seam from WS to set sts.

Seams

With RS tog, pin sleeve top into armhole, matching straight edge of sleeve to straight edge of armhole and excluding the armhole BO. Working with the WS of the sleeve facing you and the garment body away from you, use the slip-st crochet method (see Glossary) to join sleeves to armholes. Lightly steam seam from WS to set sts. With RS facing and using the mattress st with 1-st seam allowance (see Glossary), sew 3½" (9 cm) of sleeve to armhole BO edge. Using the mattress st with ½-st seam allowance (see Glossary) and working from lower edges to armholes, sew side and sleeve seams.

Front Band

With smaller needle, CO 10 sts.

ROW 1 (RS) Sl 1 pwise with yarn in front (wyf), knit to end.

ROW 2 Knit.

Rep these 2 rows until piece measures 36" (91.5 cm) from CO, or slightly less than the length of the garment from lower edge to the neck BO. Pin the non-slipped-st edge of the band to the right center front, stretching the band just slightly to eliminate ripples. With yarn threaded on a tapestry needle and using the mattress st with ½-st seam allowance and catching a garter-st bar on the edge of the band, sew band to center front. When you are close to the neck BO, add or remove rows of the band to end with Row 2 at the front neck BO.

NEXT ROW Sl 1 pwise wyf, k9, pick up and knit 10 sts across right front neck BO—20 sts.

Knit 1 (WS) row.

NEXT ROW Sl 1 pwise wyf, knit to end.

Rep the last 2 rows until band measures 2½" (6.5 cm) from pick-up, ending with a WS row.

NEXT ROW Slipping the first st, BO 10 sts, knit to end—10 sts rem.

Keeping in patt, work even until band measures 7½" (19 cm) from BO, ending with a WS row. Pin band to right neckline and, using mattress st with ½-st seam allowance, sew it in place to the shoulder seam.

NEXT ROW (RS) Sl 1 pwise wyf, k8, sl 1 kwise with yarn in back (wyb), pick up and knit 1 st in the back neck BO edge, psso—still 10 sts.

Knit 1 row. Rep the last 2 rows 18 more

button self shank

To make a button shank, insert threaded tapestry needle from WS of fabric through one hole in button and loosely back to WS of fabric through the next hole. Place a size U.S. 1 or 2 (2.25 or 2.75 mm) dpn between button and sewing yarn. Rep once in same holes, then rep 2 times for any rem pair of holes. Bring needle to RS of work behind the button (not through the button), remove dpn, lay down the threaded needle, and with cotton yarn held close to button, wind the yarn around the button sts several times to create a shank between the garment and the back of the button. Insert needle to WS, tie a square knot with other end to secure, and weave in ends.

times across back neck to left shoulder seam. Rep Rows 1 and 2 of patt until piece measures 7½" (19 cm) from left shoulder seam, ending with Row 2 of patt. With RS facing, use the cable method (see Glossary) to CO 10 sts—20 sts. Rep Rows 1 and 2 of patt until piece measures 2½" (6.5 cm) from cable CO, ending with a RS row.

NEXT ROW (WS) BO 10 sts, knit to end—10 sts rem.

Rep Rows 1 and 2 of patt until piece measures 36" (91.5 cm) from left neck BO, or slightly less than the length of the garment from the left neck BO to the lower edge. Pin band to left front neckline, neck BO edge, and center front. Use a mattress st with ½-st seam allowance to sew band to garment, adding or subtracting rows as necessary to achieve a perfect fit, ending with Row 2 of patt. BO all band sts.

Use a mattress st with ½-st seam allowance to sew band onto garment left neckline and left center front.

Attach Button

Mark button placement on right front about 7" (18 cm) down from shoulder on garter neckband, close to seam to lace. With cotton yarn threaded on a tapestry needle, sew button onto garment, making a self shank (see box at left) if button does not have its own shank.

Closure

With dpn, CO 3 sts. Work 3-st I-cord (see Glossary) until piece measures 11" (28 cm) from CO.

NEXT ROW Sl 1 kwise wyb, k2tog, psso—1 st rem.

Cut yarn, leaving an 18" (45.5 cm) tail. Pull tail through rem st to secure. Fold cord in half and overlap the right half over the left to make a large loop that will accommodate the button (slip this loop over the button to check for accuracy in size). Pin for placement on a diagonal, with overlap close to the corner of the left center front neck. Make two small decorative loops on each side of the large button loop as shown below. Pin in place and with yarn threaded on a tapestry needle and working from the WS of garment, use the whipstitch (see Glossary) to sew in place. Weave in loose ends. Lightly steam WS of closure to set sts.

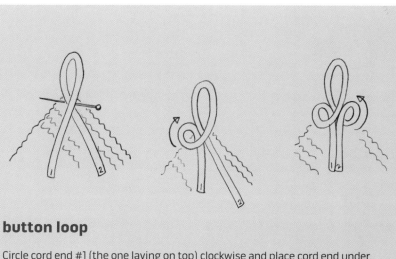

button loop

Circle cord end #1 (the one laying on top) clockwise and place cord end under, and circle cord end #2 counterclockwise and place cord end over, making sure the loops are the same size and aligning the ends.

tokai tomoshibi

FINISHED SIZE

About 42½ (49½, 56½)" (108 [125.5, 143.5] cm) bust circumference—39¾ (46¾, 53¾)" garment plus a 2¾" (7 cm) gap at center front—and about 27 (28, 29)" (68.5 [71, 73.5] cm) in length. Kimono shown measures 49½" (125.5 cm).

YARN

DK weight (#3 Light).

Shown here: Stacy Charles Ritratto (28% mohair, 53% rayon, 10% nylon, 9% polyester; 198 yd [181 m]/50 g): #14 black/bright multi, 9 (10, 11) balls.

NEEDLES

Body and sleeves: size U.S. 6 (4 mm): 24" (60 cm) circular (cir).

Garter ridges: size U.S. 5 (3.75 mm): 24" (60 cm) cir.

Adjust needle size if necessary to obtain the correct gauge.

NOTIONS

Markers (m); waste yarn or stitch holders; tapestry needle.

GAUGE

23 stitches and 30 rows = 4" (10 cm) in fan stitch on larger needle.

Glossy rayon fiber winks like city lights on a dark mohair ground in the yarn I chose for this dressy kimono. Historically, black was not often used in the Japanese color palette, except to symbolize sorrow and bereavement. In contemporary life, both Eastern and Western, black is a wardrobe staple and is a bold expression of sophistication. The sparks of color in this black kimono visually lighten the aura and exponentially expand ensemble possibilities. Wear it over richly saturated colors such as the brilliant teal Ao (page 38) to magnify the rich bits of color in the yarn.

Fans are widely used in Japanese life, from small personal ones to large exquisitely painted works of art for interior walls. I used a pattern with a stylized fan motif to add a subtle overall texture to this garment. Lace openwork at the hem and sleeve cuffs affords a lovely counterpoint. Light as air, this gossamer kimono is magical.

stitch guide

CHEVRON LACE PATTERN
(multiple of 7 sts + 2)

ROW 1 (RS) K1, *k1, k2tog, yo, k1, yo, ssk, k1; rep from * to last st, k1.

ROW 2 Purl.

ROW 3 K1, *k2tog, yo, k3, yo, ssk; rep from * to last st, k1

ROW 4 Purl.

Repeat Rows 1–4 for pattern.

FAN STITCH
(multiple of 10 sts + 2)

ROWS 1–12 Work in St st.

ROW 13 (RS) K1, *insert needle into st 4 rows below third st on left needle, draw through a loop long enough to span the 4 rows without pulling, leave loop on right needle, k3, draw a loop through same st (4 rows below), k2, then make a third long loop into same st (4 rows below), k5; rep from * to last st, k1.

ROW 14 P1, *p5, purl long loop and next st tog, p1, purl long loop and next st tog, p1, ssp (purling next st and long loop tog so long loop lays on top; see Glossary); rep from * to last st, p1.

ROWS 15–26 Work in St st (12 rows).

ROW 27 K1, *k5, insert right needle into st 4 rows below third st on left needle and draw a loop through, k3, draw a loop through same st (4 rows below), k2, then make a third long loop into same st (4 rows below); rep from * to last st, k1.

ROW 28 P1, *purl long loop and next st tog, p1, purl long loop and next st tog, p1, ssp, p5; rep from * to last st, p1.

Repeat Rows 1–28 for pattern.

Back

With larger needle, CO 121 (142, 163) sts. Do not join. Work chevron lace patt (see Stitch Guide) until piece measures about 3" (7.5 cm) from CO, ending with Row 3 of patt. Change to smaller needle and purl 1 row. Knit 4 rows—2 garter ridges. Knit 1 row, inc 1 (inc 0, dec 1) st—122 (142, 162) sts. Change to larger needle and purl 1 row. Work fan st (see Stitch Guide) until piece measures 27 (28, 29)" (68.5 [71, 73.5] cm) from CO, ending with a WS row. Place all sts on waste yarn holder.

Fronts (make 2)

With larger needle, CO 44 (51, 58) sts. Do not join. Work chevron lace patt until piece measures about 3" (7.5 cm) from CO, ending with Row 3 of patt. Change to smaller needle and purl 1 row, then knit 4 rows—2 garter ridges. Knit 1 row, dec 2 (inc 1, inc 4) st(s) evenly spaced—42 (52, 62) sts. Change to larger needle and purl 1 row. Change to fan st and work even until piece measures 27 (28, 29)" (68.5 [71, 73.5] cm) from CO, ending with a WS row. Place all sts on waste yarn holder.

Right Sleeve

With larger needle, CO 52 sts (for lower edge of the front of the sleeve). Do not join. Work fan st until piece measures 30 (32, 34)" (76 [81.5, 86.5] cm) from CO, ending with a WS row. BO all sts (this is the lower edge of the back of the sleeve).

Edging

With smaller needle and RS facing, pick up and knit 170 (184, 198) sts evenly

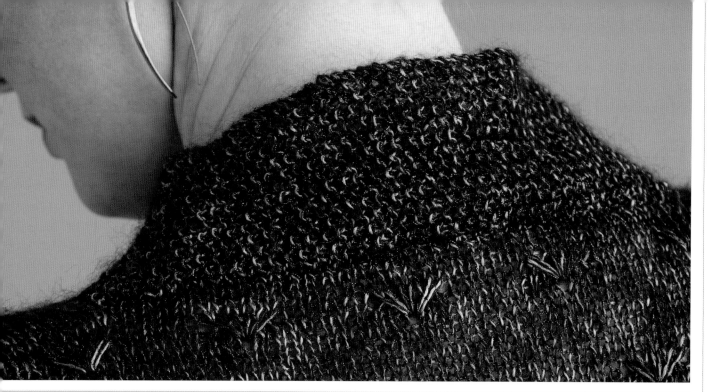

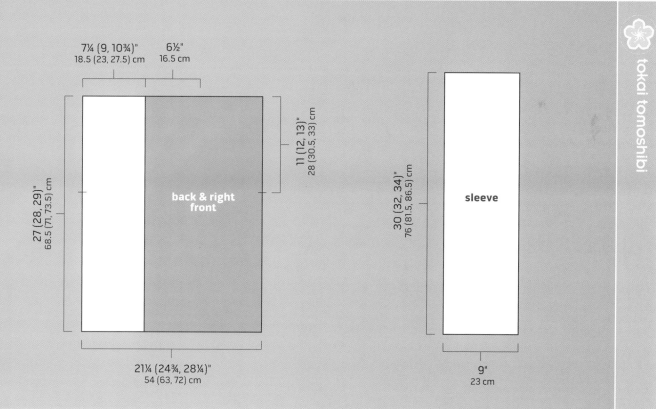

7¼ (9, 10¾)"
18.5 (23, 27.5) cm

6½"
16.5 cm

11 (12, 13)"
28 (30.5, 33) cm

back & right front

27 (28, 29)"
68.5 (71, 73.5) cm

21¼ (24¾, 28¼)"
54 (63, 72) cm

30 (32, 34)"
76 (81.5, 86.5) cm

sleeve

9"
23 cm

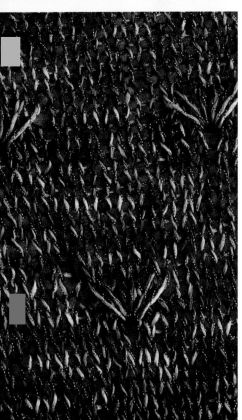

spaced along right-hand selvedge edge. Knit 2 rows. With WS facing, BO all sts—2 garter ridges on RS. With smaller needle and RS facing, pick up and knit 170 (184, 198) sts evenly spaced along left-hand selvedge edge. Knit 3 rows. Work Row 1 of chevron lace patt. Change to larger needle and cont in chevron lace patt for about 2½" (6.5 cm), ending with Row 4 of patt. BO all sts in k1, p1 rib.

Left Sleeve

CO and work as for right sleeve.

Edging

With smaller needle and RS facing, pick up and knit 170 (184, 198) sts evenly spaced along left-hand selvedge edge. Knit 2 rows. With WS facing, BO all sts—2 garter ridges on RS. With smaller needle and RS facing, pick up and knit 170 (184, 198) sts evenly spaced along right-hand selvedge edge. Knit 3 rows. Work Row 1 of chevron lace patt. Change to larger needle and cont in chevron lace patt for about 2½" (6.5 cm), ending with Row 4 of patt. BO all sts in k1, p1 rib.

Finishing

Weave in loose ends. Wet-block (see Glossary) all pieces to measurements. Let dry completely.

Join Shoulders

Place 122 (142, 162) held back sts onto one needle and 42 (52, 62) held right front sts onto another needle. With RS tog and larger needle, use the three-needle method (see Glossary) to BO 42 (52, 62) right front and back sts tog for right shoulder, then BO next 38 sts for back neck, then place 42 (52, 62) held left front sts onto second needle and use the three-needle method to BO 42 (52, 62) left front and rem back sts tog for left shoulder.

Neckband

With smaller needle, CO 15 sts. Work in seed st as foll:

ROW 1 *K1, p1; rep from * to last st, k1.

Rep this row until piece measures 59 (61, 63)" (150 [155, 160] cm) from CO. BO all sts in patt. With yarn threaded on a tapestry needle, sew neckband to garment, using a mattress st with 1-st seam allowance (see Glossary) on garment and catching purl sts on the seed st edge of the neckband. Steam-block lightly to set sts.

Seams

With yarn threaded on a tapestry needle and using a mattress st with 1-st seam allowance, sew side seams for 16" (40.5 cm) from lower edge. Use horizontal-to-horizontal grafting (see Glossary) to join CO to BO edges of sleeves. Lightly steam-block to set sts. Align midpoint of sleeve top with shoulder seam and pin sleeve to garment body for 9 (10, 11)" (23 [25.5, 28] cm) down from shoulder on both front and back (bottom of sleeve will remain free). Sew sleeve in place.

Steam-block lightly to set sts.

shiro shiriku

FINISHED SIZE

About 36 (40½, 44, 48, 52)" (91.5 [103, 112, 122, 132] cm) in circumference and 21 (21, 22, 23, 23)" (53.5 [53.5, 56, 58.5, 58.5] cm) in length. Top shown measures 40½" (103 cm).

YARN

Worsted weight (#4 Medium).

Shown here: South West Trading Company Phoenix (100% soysilk; 175 yd [160 m]/100 g): #098 white, 4 (5, 5, 6, 6) balls.

NEEDLES

Size U.S. 7 (4.5 mm): 24" (60 cm) circular (cir).

Adjust needle size if necessary to obtain the correct gauge.

NOTIONS

Size G/6 (4.5 mm) crochet hook; tapestry needle.

GAUGE

19 stitches and 24 rows = 4" (10 cm) in stockinette stitch.

NOTES

This top is knitted primarily in stockinette stitch with garter ridges created by knitting wrong-side rows.

The stockinette stitch at the neck edge will naturally roll toward the right side to create a soft finish.

Shiro, or white, was basic to Heian color fashion. Placed on top or underneath, white expanded the color impression of other coordinating layers. Symbolically, white represented purity and beginnings. A new empress would wear a white jacket at her investiture ceremony and a soon-to-be new mother would wear white robes.

The natural white of the soysilk ribbon yarn I used for this design is timeless and will coordinate with virtually any color in the rainbow. The randomly spaced garter-stitch textural stripes on a stockinette-stitch background pay homage to the many variations of stripes woven into kimono through the centuries. Stripes are always a sophisticated aesthetic.

Once blocked, the graceful flow of this garment is more pronounced, but it also measures a bit larger than the final knitted measurement. Be sure to account for this additional ease when choosing the appropriate size.

Back

CO 86 (96, 104, 114, 123) sts. Do not join. Work in St st until piece measures 3" (7.5 cm) from CO, ending with a RS row. Knit 1 (WS) row to make a garter ridge on RS. Work in St st until piece measures 1½" (3.8 cm) from garter ridge, ending with a RS row. Knit 1 (WS) row to make another garter ridge on RS. Work in St st until piece measures 2" (5 cm) from previous ridge, ending with a RS row. Knit the next 3 rows to create 2 garter ridges on RS. Work in St st until piece measures 1" (2.5 cm) from previous ridge, ending with a RS row. Knit 1 (WS) row to make another garter ridge. Work in St st until piece measures 2¼" (5.5 cm) from previous ridge, ending with a RS row. Knit 1

(WS) row to make another garter ridge. Work in St st until piece measures ½" (1.3 cm) from previous ridge, ending with a RS row. Knit 1 (WS) row to make another garter ridge. Work in St st until piece measures 1" (2.5 cm) from previous ridge, ending with a RS row. Knit 1 (WS) row to make another garter ridge—8 garter ridges total. Work even in St st until piece measures 14 (14, 14½, 15, 15)" (35.5 [35.5, 37, 38, 38] cm) from CO, ending with a WS row.

Shape Armholes

NOTE *Garter ridges are worked at the same time as armhole shaping; read the foll section all the way through before proceeding.*

BO 2 (2, 2, 5, 5) sts at beg of next 2 rows—82 (92, 100, 104, 113) sts rem. Dec 1 st each end of needle on next 2 (2, 2, 4, 8) RS rows—78 (88, 96, 96, 97) sts rem. *At the same time* when piece measures 3" (7.5 cm) from previous ridge, ending with a RS row, knit 1 (WS) row to make another garter ridge. Work in St st until piece measures 1" (2.5 cm) from previous ridge, ending with a RS row. Knit the next 5 rows to create 3 garter ridges on RS. Work in St st until piece measures 1¼" (3.2 cm) from previous ridge, ending with a RS row. Knit 1 (WS) row to create another garter ridge—13 garter ridges total. Work in St st until armholes measure 7 (7, 7½, 8, 8)" (18 [18, 19, 20.5, 20.5] cm), ending with a WS row. BO all sts.

Front

CO and work same as back.

Finishing

Block to measurements. Weave in loose ends.

Seams

With RS tog, pin shoulders tog. Using the slip-st crochet method (see Glossary) and beg at armhole edge, join shoulders for 2½ (3½, 4¼, 4¼, 4¼)" (6.5 [9, 11, 11, 11] cm). With yarn threaded on a tapestry needle and using the mattress st with ½-st seam allowance (see Glossary), sew side seams.

Steam seams lightly to set sts.

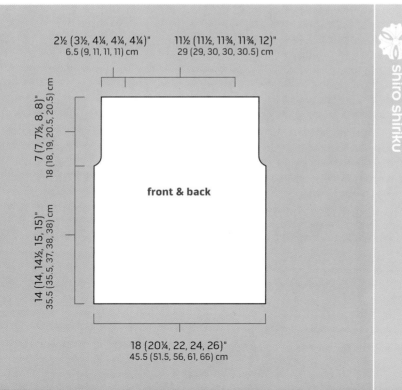

2½ (3½, 4¼, 4¼, 4¼)"
6.5 (9, 11, 11, 11) cm

11½ (11½, 11¾, 11¾, 12)"
29 (29, 30, 30, 30.5) cm

7 (7, 7½, 8, 8)"
18 (18, 19, 20.5, 20.5) cm

front & back

14 (14, 14½, 15, 15)"
35.5 (35.5, 37, 38, 38) cm

18 (20¼, 22, 24, 26)"
45.5 (51.5, 56, 61, 66) cm

shiriku tsui-do

FINISHED SIZE
About 44 (48, 52)" (112 [122, 132] cm) circumference and 25 (26, 27)" (63.5 [66, 68.5] cm) in length. Kimono shown measures 48" (122 cm).

YARN
Worsted weight (#4 Medium).

Shown here: Rowan Summer Tweed (70% silk, 30% cotton; 118 yd [108 m]/50 g): #537 summer berry (MC), 11 (12, 13) skeins; #507 rush (pale green; CC), 2 skeins.

NEEDLES
Size U.S. 8 (5 mm): 24" (60 cm) circular (cir) plus spare needle same size or smaller for three-needle BO.

Adjust needle size if necessary to obtain the correct gauge.

NOTIONS
Stitch holders; marker (m); removable markers; tapestry needle; knitting pins.

GAUGE
16 stitches and 24 rows = 4" (10 cm) in stockinette stitch.

The combination of akai (red), for passion, and *moegi* (a variety of green), for a restful and fresh feel, are a paradox in the color palette that create exciting color vibration. In Western color wheel terms, they are complementary, or opposites—a relationship that never fails to electrify each color. Among the many colors that are favored for Japanese kimono in the summer months are red, dead-leaf yellow, and sprout green. For this garment, I've chosen a soft red of medium value and intensity and a pale celery green for subtle embroidery to make it a year-round staple. Some of the most artistic surface embellishment comes from the historic folk textiles of commoners. In straightforward manner, running-stitch embroidery brings designs and images to life.

This silk tweed yarn has a very tactile surface texture with the appearance of raw woven silk, yet is soft to the touch. This length of kimono is versatility at its best—it can adapt to most skirt lengths and any pants. Enjoy!

stitch guide

SEED STITCH
(even number of sts)

ROW 1 (RS) *K1, p1; rep from *.

ROW 2 *P1, k1; rep from *.

Repeat Rows 1 and 2 for pattern.

Back

With MC, CO 88 (96, 104) sts. Do not join. Knit 4 rows. Work in seed st (see Stitch Guide) until piece measures 2" (5 cm) from CO, ending with a WS row. Change to St st and work even until piece measures 25 (26, 27)" (63.5 [66, 68.5] cm) from CO. Place sts on holder.

Right Front

With MC, CO 52 (56, 60) sts. Knit 4 rows. Work in seed st until piece measures 2" (5 cm) from CO, ending with a WS row. Set up front border as foll:

ROW 1 (RS) [K1, p1] 3 times, k1, place marker (pm), knit to end.

ROW 2 Purl to m, [k1, p1] 3 times, k1.

Rep these 2 rows until piece measures 6" (15 cm) from CO, ending with a WS row.

Shape Neck

DEC ROW (RS) K1, work k2tog or p2tog as necessary to maintain seed st patt, work to end of row—1 st dec'd.

NEXT ROW Purl to m, work seed st to last st, p1.

Maintaining seed st at center front, dec 1 st at neck edge in this manner every 6th row 18 (19, 19) more times, working decs as (k1, ssk, knit to end) after all seed sts have been dec'd—33 (36, 40) sts rem. Work even in St st until piece measures 25 (26, 27)" (63.5 [66, 68.5] cm) from CO. Place sts on holder.

Left Front

With MC, CO 52 (56, 60) sts. Knit 4 rows. Work in seed st until piece measures 2" (5 cm) from CO, ending with a WS row. Set up front border as foll:

ROW 1 (RS) Knit to last 7 sts, pm, [k1, p1] 3 times, k1.

ROW 2 [K1, p1] 3 times, k1, purl to end. Rep these 2 rows until piece measures 6" (15 cm) from CO, ending with a WS row.

Shape Neck

DEC ROW (RS) Knit to m, work in seed st to last 3 sts, work k2tog or p2tog as necessary to maintain seed st patt, k1—1 st dec'd.

NEXT ROW P1, work in seed st to m, purl to end.

Maintaining seed st at center front, dec 1 st at neck edge in this manner every 6th row 18 (19, 19) more times, working decs as (knit to last 3 sts, k2tog, k1) after all seed sts have been dec'd—33 (36, 40) sts rem. Work even in St st until piece measures 25 (26, 27)" (63.5 [66, 68.5] cm) from CO. Place sts on holder.

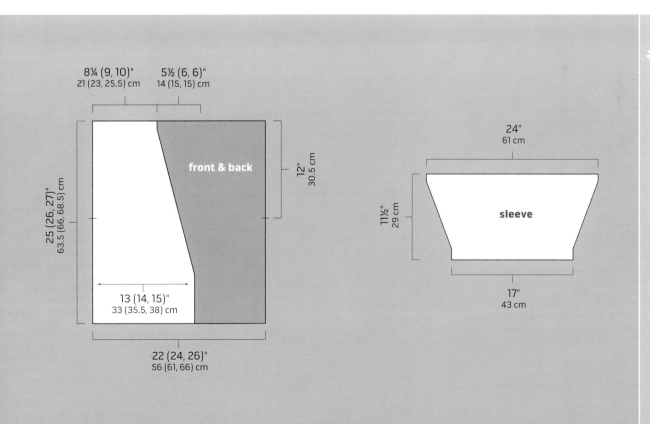

8¼ (9, 10)"
21 (23, 25.5) cm

5½ (6, 6)"
14 (15, 15) cm

front & back

12"
30.5 cm

25 (26, 27)"
63.5 (66, 68.5) cm

13 (14, 15)"
33 (35.5, 38) cm

22 (24, 26)"
56 (61, 66) cm

24"
61 cm

sleeve

11½"
29 cm

17"
43 cm

Join Shoulders

Place 88 (96, 104) held back sts onto one needle and 33 (36, 40) right front sts onto a second needle. With RS tog, use the three-needle method (see Glossary) to BO 33 (36, 40) right front and back sts tog for right shoulder, then BO next 22 (24, 24) back sts for back neck, then place 33 (36, 40) left front sts onto second needle and BO 33 (36, 40) left front sts tog with rem back sts for left shoulder. Cut yarn and pull tail through rem st to secure.

Sleeves

Measure 12" (30.5 cm) down from shoulder seam on front and back at side edges and mark for sleeve placement. With RS facing, pick up and knit 96 sts between markers. Do not join. Knit 1 (WS) row—1 garter ridge on RS. Work in St st for 4 rows.

DEC ROW: (RS) K1, ssk, knit to last 3 sts, k2tog, k1—2 sts dec'd.

Rep dec row every 4th row 13 more times—68 sts rem. Work even if necessary until piece measures 10" (25.5 cm) from pick-up row, ending with a WS row. Work in seed st for 1¼" (3.2 cm), ending with a RS row. Knit 2 rows. With WS facing, BO all sts.

Finishing

Neckband

With RS facing and beg at right center front at beg of decs 6" (15 cm) above CO edge, pick up and knit 72 (76, 80) sts along right front edge, 22 (24, 24) sts across back neck, and 72 (76, 80) sts along left front edge to point 6"

(15 cm) above CO edge on left front—166 (176, 184) sts total. Knit 1 (WS) row for garter ridge. Work in seed st until neckband measures 1¼" (3.2 cm) from garter ridge, ending with a WS row. Knit 2 rows. With RS facing, BO all sts.

Embroidery

Mark center back with knitting pin. Thread tapestry needle with about 5 yd (4.5 m) of CC. Leaving a 6" (15 cm) tail, insert needle from WS about ½" (1.3 cm) to the left of the pin and about ½" (1.3 cm) down from top of back. Work running sts (see Glossary) vertically for 8" (20.5 cm), then work horizontally to about ½" (1.3 cm) from side edge, then work vertically to about ½" (1.3 cm) from top of back, then horizontally toward center back, ending ½" (1.3 cm) shy of first line of running sts. Work concentric rectangles in this manner, spacing the rectangles ½" (1.3 cm) apart as shown in the stitching diagram below. Weave in loose ends on WS. Make similar concentric rectangles for right shoulder, beg 1" (2.5 cm) from lower right corner of first rectangle. Make similar concentric rectangles for lower center back measuring about 5" (12.5 cm) wide and 8" (20.5 cm) long, beg about 1" (2.5 cm) below upper rectangles. Make similar concentric rectangles for left and right fronts.

Seams

With yarn threaded on a tapestry needle, use a mattress st with ½-st seam allowance (see Glossary) to sew side and sleeve seams.

Weave in loose ends. Block, using the wet-towel method (see Glossary).

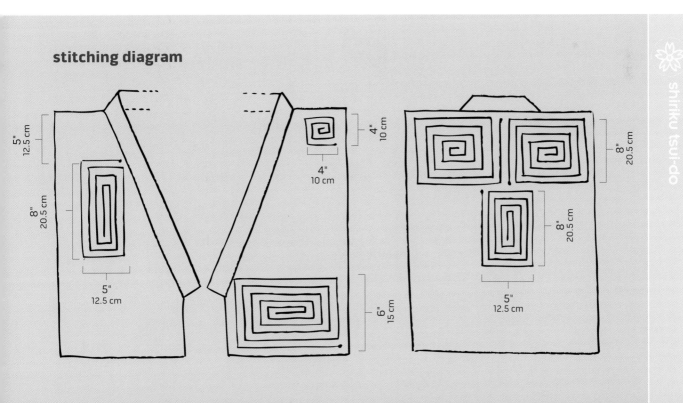

stitching diagram

kumo

FINISHED SIZE

About 49" (124.5 cm) in circumference and about 28" (71 cm) in length.

YARN

Worsted weight (#4 Medium).

Shown here: Berroco Bonsai (97% bamboo, 3% nylon; 77 yd [70 m]/50 g): #4152 kaigun (purple; MC), 20 skeins; #4103 bamboo (tan; CC), 1 skein.

NEEDLES

Body and sleeves: size U.S. 7 (4.5 mm): 24" (60 cm) circular (cir). *Neckband:* size U.S. 6 (4 mm): two 29" (73.5 cm) cir.

Adjust needle size if necessary to obtain the correct gauge.

NOTIONS

Stitch holders; removable markers; tapestry needle; light-colored sewing thread; size H/8 (5 mm) crochet hook for embroidery.

GAUGE

18 stitches and 24 rows = 4" (10 cm) in stockinette stitch on larger needle.

NOTE

Instructions for the white shell are provided on page 126.

Kanbun kosode was a kimono style of dramatic asymmetrical imagery that trailed in bold fashion from right shoulder to lower left hem. Genroku was a brief time in Japanese history (1688–1704) that represented the zenith of this visual drama. I have followed that aesthetic in this kimono with stylized cloud forms—a nature reference that spans the seasons—but I've taken artistic license by sweeping my diagonal in the other direction.

The blue ribbon yarn I used for this kimono is reminiscent of indigo, but of a lightened, faded shade. Indigo is a common dyestuff for the peasantry, but the glossy sheen of the ribbon yarn produces a garment suitable for royalty—a poetic paradox. The cloud imagery, worked in crochet-chain embroidery, is worked mostly on the back. While this surface design is decidedly Japanese, you may opt for a plain kimono. This yarn produces a knitted fabric of such glorious drape that it is a work of art even without embellishment.

Back

With MC and larger needle, CO 110 sts. Do not join. Purl 1 WS foundation row. Work even in St st (knit RS rows; purl WS rows) until piece measures 28" (71 cm) from CO, ending with a WS row. Place sts on holder.

Right Front

With MC and larger needle, CO 60 sts. Do not join. Purl 1 WS foundation row. Work even in St st until piece measures 8" (20.5 cm) from CO, ending with a WS row.

Shape Neck

DEC ROW (RS) K1, ssk, knit to end—1 st dec'd.

Work 5 rows even in St st. Rep the last 6 rows 19 more times—40 sts rem. Cont even until piece measures 28" (71 cm) from CO, ending with a WS row. Place sts on holder.

Left Front

CO and work as for right front until piece measures 8" (20.5 cm) from CO, ending with a WS row.

Shape Neck

DEC ROW (RS) Knit to last 3 sts, k2tog, k1—1 st dec'd.

Work 5 rows even in St st. Rep the last 6 rows 19 more times—40 sts rem. Cont

even until piece measures 28" (71 cm) from CO, ending with a WS row. Place sts on holder.

Join Shoulders

Place 110 held back sts onto one needle and 40 held right front sts onto another needle. With MC, larger needle, and RS tog, use the three-needle method (see Glossary) to BO 40 right front and 40 back sts tog for right shoulder, then BO the next 30 back sts as usual, then place 40 held left front sts onto second needle and BO 40 left front sts tog with rem 40 back sts for left shoulder.

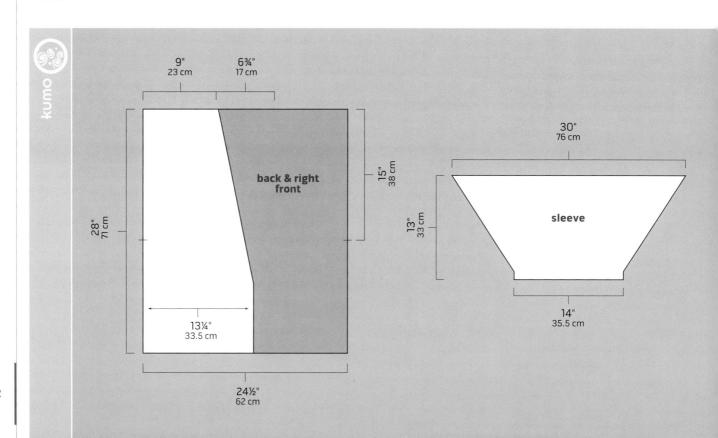

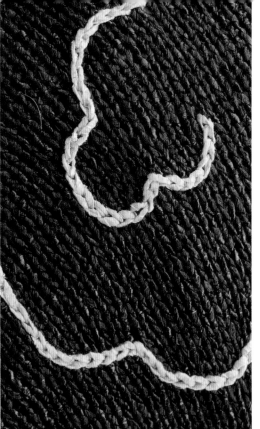

Sleeves

Measure and mark 15" (38 cm) down from each shoulder on front and back at each side edge. With MC, larger needle, and RS facing, pick up and knit 135 sts evenly spaced between markers. Knit 1 WS row—1 garter ridge on RS.

DEC ROW (RS) K1, ssk, knit to last 3 sts, k2tog, k1—2 sts dec'd.

Work 1 WS row even. Rep the last 2 rows 35 more times—63 sts rem. Cont even in St st until piece measures 13" (33 cm) from garter ridge, ending with a WS row. BO all sts.

Finishing

Neckband
With MC, smaller needle, RS facing, and beg at lower center front corner, pick up and knit 116 sts along right front edge, 30 sts across back neck, and 116 sts along left front edge—262 sts total. Working back and forth with 2 cir needles and slipping the first st of every row kwise, work garter st (knit every row) for 12 rows—6 garter ridges on RS; neckband measures about 1¼" (3.2 cm). Change to St st and work for ¾" (2 cm) longer, ending with a WS row. BO all sts.

Wet-block (see Glossary) pieces in a single layer to measurements. Let air-dry completely.

Seams
With MC threaded on a tapestry needle and using the mattress st with ½-st seam allowance (see Glossary), sew side and sleeve seams.

Crochet Chain Embroidery
Enlarge the cloud embroidery diagram below if necessary. With light-colored sewing thread, sew loose basting sts to indicate cloud shapes. With CC and a crochet hook, work crochet chain embroidery (see Glossary) along basting. Remove basting thread.

Weave in loose ends and steam lightly to set sts.

cloud embroidery diagram

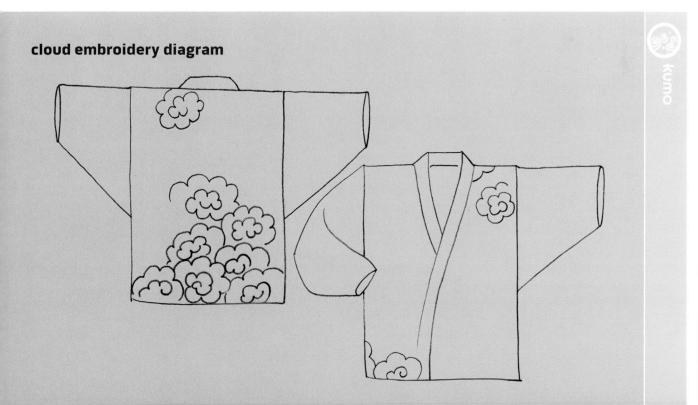

under kosode shell

FINISHED SIZE

About 37½ (41, 44½, 47½, 51)" (95 [104, 113, 120.5, 129.5] cm) in circumference and 21 (23, 24, 25, 26)" (53.5 [58.5, 61, 63.5, 66] cm) in length. Shell shown measures 37½" (95 cm).

YARN

Sportweight (#2 Fine).

Shown here: Plymouth Ecco Silk (100% silk; 148 yd [135 m]/50 g): #100 natural, 5 (6, 7, 8, 8) skeins.

NEEDLES

Body and sleeves: size U.S. 5 (3.75 mm): 24" (60 cm) circular (cir) and 2 double-pointed (dpn) for three-needle bind-off.
Edging: size U.S. 4 (3.5 mm): 24" (60 cm) cir.

Adjust needle size if necessary to obtain the correct gauge.

NOTIONS

Markers (m); stitch holders or waste yarn; tapestry needle.

GAUGE

24 stitches and 28 rows = 4" (10 cm) in stockinette stitch on larger needle.

Kosode was the prototype for kimono, translated as "small sleeves," which referred to small sleeve openings, not narrow circumference. Initially, kosode was worn as the innermost robe. Early in Heian history, this first undergarment layer was almost always an undyed natural color in a plain-weave silk. Each kosode, or kimono, was worn lapped left over right to provide a stunning color sequence along the overlapping V-neck.

In this simplified sleeveless shell design, I employed an unusual construction for the overlapping V-neck that is fun to work and stabilizes the stress point of the V. The streamlined design is only minimally textured with an eyelet rib at the lower edge. The silk yarn I used is as soft as luxury lingerie and will certainly feel like a first undergarment layer, but it can be worn equally well on its own. Try this shell under the Kumo kimono (page 120) to define your own mode of elegance.

Back

With smaller needle and using the cable method (see Glossary), CO 113 (123, 133, 143, 153) sts. Do not join.

ROW 1 (RS) *P1, k1 through back loop (k1tbl), p1, k2; rep from * to last 3 sts, p1, k1tbl, p1.

ROW 2 K1, p1 through back loop (p1tbl), k1, *p2, k1, p1tbl, k1; rep from *.

ROW 3 *P1, k1tbl, p1, k1, yo, k1; rep from * to last 3 sts, p1, k1tbl, p1—135 (147, 159, 171, 183) sts.

ROW 4 K1, p1tbl, k1, *p3, k1, p1tbl, k1; rep from *.

ROW 5 *P1, k1tbl, p1, k3, pass 3rd st on right needle over first 2 sts; rep from * to last 3 sts, p1, k1tbl, p1—113 (123, 133, 143, 153) sts rem.

ROW 6 Rep Row 2.

Change to larger needle and work even in St st until piece measures 13 (14½, 15, 15½, 16)" (33 [37, 38, 39.5, 40.5] cm) from CO, ending with a WS row.

Shape Armholes

BO 5 sts at beg of next 2 rows, then BO 2 sts at beg of foll 2 rows—99 (109, 119, 129, 139) sts rem.

DEC ROW (RS) Sl 1 pwise with yarn in back (wyb), p1tbl, ssk, knit to last 4 sts, k2tog, p1tbl, k1—2 sts dec'd.

NEXT ROW Sl 1 pwise with yarn in front (wyf), k1tbl, purl to last 2 sts, k1tbl, p1. Rep the last 2 rows 6 (7, 9, 11, 14) more times—85 (93, 99, 105, 109) sts rem. Work even in St st until armholes measure 7½ (8, 8½, 9, 9½)" (19 [20.5, 21.5, 23, 24] cm), ending with a WS row.

Shape Shoulders

Work short-rows (see Glossary) as foll:

SHORT-ROW 1 (RS) K75 (81, 86, 91, 95), wrap next st, turn.

SHORT-ROW 2 (WS) P65 (69, 73, 77, 81), wrap next st, turn.

SHORT-ROW 3 K54 (57, 60, 63, 66), wrap next st, turn.

SHORT-ROW 4 P43 (45, 47, 49, 51), wrap next st, turn.

NEXT ROW (RS) Knit to end, working wraps tog with wrapped sts.

NEXT ROW (WS) Purl to end, working wraps tog with wrapped sts.

Place sts on holder.

Front

CO and work as for back until piece measures 10½ (12, 12½, 13, 13½)" (26.5 [30.5, 31.5, 33, 34.5] cm) from CO, ending with a WS row—113 (123, 133, 143, 153) sts.

Shape Left Neck and Armhole

NOTE *Armhole shaping is introduced as neck shaping is worked; read the next sections all the way through before proceeding.*

With RS facing, k49 (54, 59, 64, 69), BO 13 sts, place next 50 (55, 60, 65, 70) sts on holder to work later for right neck—50 (55, 60, 65, 70) sts rem; 49 (54, 59, 64, 69) left neck sts plus 1 st rem from BO.

NEXT ROW (WS) Sl 1 pwise wyf (st rem from BO), pick up and knit 13 sts inserting needle into only upper half of the BO sts, purl to end—63 (68, 73, 78, 83) sts.

NEXT ROW K49 (54, 59, 64, 69), place marker (pm), p1tbl, k13.

ALL WS ROWS Sl 1 pwise wyf, p12, k1tbl, slip marker (sl m), purl to end.

NECK DEC ROW (RS) Knit to 2 sts before m, k2tog, sl m, p1tbl, k13—1 neck st dec'd.

Dec 1 st at neck edge in this manner every 4th row 13 (14, 15, 16, 17) more times. *At the same time* when piece measures 13 (14½, 15, 15½, 16)" (33 [37, 38, 39.5, 40.5] cm) from CO, ending with a WS row, shape armhole as foll: BO 5 sts at beg of next RS row, then BO 2 sts at beg of foll RS row—7 armhole sts dec'd. Work 1 (WS) row.

ARMHOLE DEC ROW (RS) Sl 1 pwise wyb, p1tbl, ssk, work to end, working neck shaping as established—1 armhole st dec'd.

Working neck decs as established, dec 1 st at armhole edge in this manner every RS row 6 (7, 9, 11, 14) more times—35 (38, 40, 42, 43) sts rem when all neck and armhole shaping has been completed. Work even until armhole measures 7½ (8, 8½, 9, 9½)" (19 [20.5, 21.5, 23, 24] cm), ending with a RS row.

Shape Shoulder

SHORT-ROW 1 (WS) P25 (26, 27, 28, 29), wrap next st, turn.

SHORT-ROW 2 (RS) Knit.

SHORT-ROW 3 P14, wrap next st, turn.

SHORT-ROW 4 Knit.

NEXT ROW (WS) Purl, working wraps tog with wrapped sts.

Place 21 (24, 26, 28, 29) shoulder sts on one holder and 14 neckband sts on another holder.

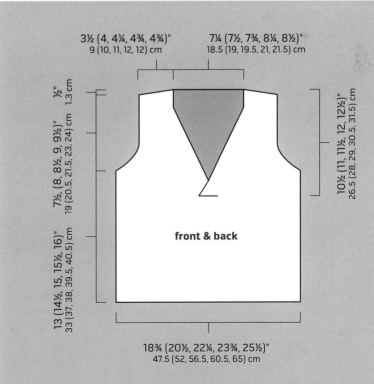

3½ (4, 4¼, 4¾, 4¾)"
9 (10, 11, 12, 12) cm

7¼ (7½, 7¾, 8¼, 8½)"
18.5 (19, 19.5, 21, 21.5) cm

½" 1.3 cm

7½, (8, 8½, 9, 9½)"
19 (20.5, 21.5, 23, 24) cm

13 (14½, 15, 15½, 16)"
33 (37, 38, 39.5, 40.5) cm

10½ (11, 11½, 12, 12½)"
26.5 (28, 29, 30.5, 31.5) cm

front & back

18¾ (20½, 22¼, 23¾, 25½)"
47.5 (52, 56.5, 60.5, 65) cm

Shape Right Neck

NOTE *Armhole shaping is introduced as neck shaping is worked; read the next sections all the way through before proceeding.* Place 50 (55, 60, 65, 70) held right neck sts onto needle. With RS facing, fold left front forward toward hem to reveal WS sts. Join yarn and pick up and knit 13 sts in purl bars behind and below BO sts of left front, p1tbl, pm, knit to end—63 (68, 73, 78, 83) sts.

NEXT ROW (WS) P49 (54, 59, 64, 69), sl m, k1tbl, p13.

NEXT ROW Sl 1 pwise wyb, k12, p1tbl, sl m, knit to end.

NEXT ROW Purl to m, sl m, k1tbl, p13.

NECK DEC ROW (RS) Sl 1 pwise wyb, k12, p1tbl, sl m, ssk, knit to end—1 neck st dec'd.

Dec 1 st at neck edge in this manner every 4th row 13 (14, 15, 16, 17) more times. *At the same time* when piece measures 13 (14½, 15, 15½, 16)" (33 [37, 38, 39.5, 40.5] cm) from CO, ending with a RS row, shape armhole as foll: BO 5 sts at beg of next WS row, then BO 2 sts at beg of foll WS row—7 armhole sts dec'd.

ARMHOLE DEC ROW (RS) Working neckline shaping as established, work to last 4 sts, k2tog, p1tbl, k1—1 armhole st dec'd.

ALL WS ROWS Sl 1 pwise wyf, k1tbl, purl to m, sl m, k1tbl, p13.

Working neck decs as established, dec 1 st at armhole edge in this manner every RS row 6 (7, 9, 11, 14) more times—35 (38, 40, 42, 43) sts rem when all neck and armhole shaping has been completed. Work even until armhole measures 7½ (8, 8½, 9, 9½)" (19 [20.5, 21.5, 23, 24] cm), ending with a WS row.

Shape Shoulder

SHORT-ROW 1 (RS) K25 (26, 27, 28, 29), wrap next st, turn.

SHORT-ROW 2 (WS) Purl.

SHORT-ROW 3 K14, wrap next st, turn.

SHORT-ROW 4 Purl.

NEXT ROW (RS) Knit, working wraps tog with wrapped sts.

Place 21 (24, 26, 28, 29) shoulder sts on one holder and 14 neckband sts on another holder.

Finishing

Join Shoulders

Place 85 (93, 99, 105, 109) held back sts onto one needle and 21 (24, 26, 28, 29) held right front sts onto another needle. With larger needle and RS tog, use the three-needle method (see Glossary) to BO 21 (24, 26, 28, 29) right front sts tog with 21 (24, 26, 28, 29) back sts for right shoulder, then BO next 43 (45, 47, 49, 51) back sts for back neck, then place 21 (24, 26, 28, 29) held left front sts onto a dpn and BO 21 (24, 26, 28, 29) left front sts tog with rem back sts for left shoulder. Cut yarn and pull tail through rem st to secure.

Left Back Neckband

Place 14 held left front neckband sts onto larger needle.

ROW 1 (RS) P1, k13.

ROW 2 Sl 1 pwise wyf, p12, k1.

Rep these 2 rows until neckband measures about 3½ (3½, 3¾, 3¾, 4)" (9 [9, 9.5, 9.5, 10] cm) from shoulder when slightly stretched, ending with a RS row—working yarn is at sl st edge. Cut yarn, leaving a 36" (91.5 cm) tail for grafting. Place sts on holder.

Right Back Neckband

Place 14 held right front neckband sts onto larger needle.

ROW 1 (WS) K1, p13.

ROW 2 Sl 1 pwise wyb, k12, p1.

Rep these 2 rows until neckband measures about 3½ (3½, 3¾, 3¾, 4)" (9 [9, 9.5, 9.5, 10] cm) from shoulder when slightly stretched, ending with a RS row—working yarn is at seam edge of neckband.

Join Neckbands

Place each set of 14 neckband sts on a dpn. Thread tail from left front neckband onto a tapestry needle. Holding both dpns parallel with WS tog and working from sl st edge toward seam edge of neckband, use the Kitchener st (see Glossary) to graft the sts tog. With yarn threaded on a tapestry needle, use the horizontal-to-vertical seam (see Glossary) to sew neckband to back neck.

Weave in loose ends. Block, using the wet-towel method (see Glossary).

glossary

Bind-Offs
Three-Needle Bind-Off
Place the stitches to be joined onto two separate needles and hold the needles parallel so that the right sides of knitting face together. Insert a third needle into the first stitch on each of two needles **(Figure 1)** and knit them together as one stitch **(Figure 2)**, *knit the next stitch on each needle the same way, then use the left needle tip to lift the first stitch over the second and off the needle **(Figure 3)**. Repeat from * until no stitches remain on first two needles. Cut yarn and pull tail through last stitch to secure.

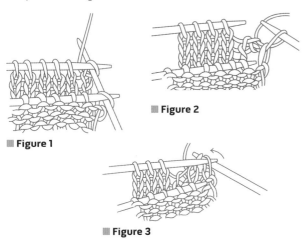

■ **Figure 2**

■ **Figure 1**

■ **Figure 3**

Blocking
Wet-Towel Blocking
Run a large bath or beach towel (or two towels for larger projects) through the rinse/spin cycle of a washing machine. Roll the knitted pieces in the wet towel(s), place the roll in a plastic bag, and leave overnight so that the knitted pieces become uniformly damp. Pin the damp pieces to a blocking surface and let air-dry thoroughly.

Cast-Ons
Backward-Loop Cast-On
*Loop working yarn and place it on needle backward so that it doesn't unwind. Repeat from *.

Cable Cast-On
Hold needle with working yarn in your left hand. *Insert right needle *between* the first two stitches on left needle **(Figure 1)**, wrap yarn around needle as if to knit, draw yarn through **(Figure 2)**, and place new loop on left needle **(Figure 3)** to form a new stitch. Repeat from * for the desired number of stitches, always working between the last two stitches on the left needle.

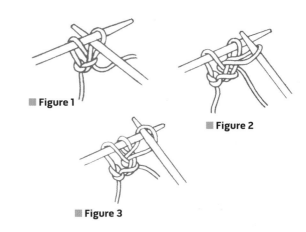

■ **Figure 1**

■ **Figure 2**

■ **Figure 3**

Crochet Chain Provisional Cast-On
With waste yarn and crochet hook, make a loose crochet chain (see page 134) about four stitches more than you need to cast on. With knitting needle, working yarn, and beginning two stitches from end of chain, pick up and knit one stitch through the back bump of each crochet chain **(Figure 1)** for desired number of stitches. When you're ready to work in the opposite direction, pull out the crochet chain to expose live stitches **(Figure 2)**.

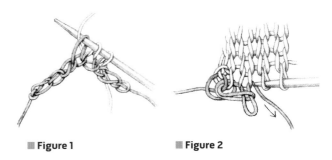

■ **Figure 1**

■ **Figure 2**

Long-Tail (Continental) Cast-On

Leaving a long tail (about ½" [1.3 cm] for each stitch to be cast on), make a slipknot and place on right needle. Place thumb and index finger of your left hand between the yarn ends so that working yarn is around your index finger and tail end is around your thumb and secure the yarn ends with your other fingers. Hold your palm upward, making a V of yarn (**Figure 1**). *Bring needle up through loop on thumb (**Figure 2**), catch first strand around index finger, and go back down through loop on thumb (**Figure 3**). Drop loop off thumb and, placing thumb back in V configuration, tighten resulting stitch on needle (**Figure 4**). Repeat from * for the desired number of stitches.

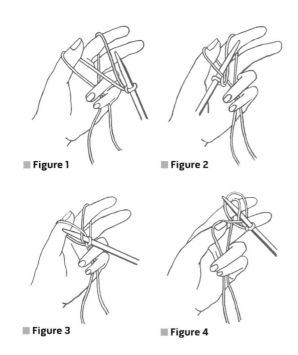

■ **Figure 1**   ■ **Figure 2**

■ **Figure 3**   ■ **Figure 4**

Crochet
Crochet Chain (ch)

Make a slipknot and place it on crochet hook if there isn't a loop already on the hook. *Yarn over hook and draw through loop on hook. Repeat from * for the desired number of stitches. To fasten off, cut yarn and draw end through last loop formed.

Single Crochet (sc)

*Insert hook into the second chain from the hook (or the next stitch), yarn over hook and draw through a loop, yarn over hook (**Figure 1**), and draw it through both loops on hook (**Figure 2**). Repeat from * for the desired number of stitches.

■ **Figure 1**   ■ **Figure 2**

Decreases
Knit 2 Together Through Back Loops (k2togtbl)

Insert right needle through the back loops of the next two stitches on the left needle, wrap the yarn around the needle, and pull a loop through while slipping the stitches off the left needle.

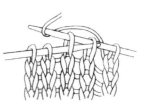

Slip, Slip, Purl (ssp)

Holding yarn in front, slip two stitches individually knitwise **(Figure 1)**, then slip these two stitches back onto left needle (they will be twisted on the needle) and purl them together through their back loops **(Figure 2)**.

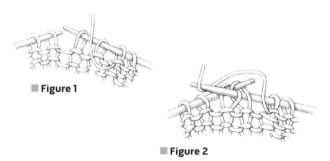

■ **Figure 1**

■ **Figure 2**

Embroidery
Crochet Chain Stitch

Holding the yarn under the fabric, insert crochet hook through the center of a knitted stitch, pull up a loop, *insert hook into the center of the next stitch along the path, pull up a second loop through the first loop on the hook. Repeat from *.

Running Stitch

Bring threaded needle in and out of fabric to form a dashed line.

I-Cord (also called Knit-Cord)

Using two double-pointed needles, cast on the desired number of stitches (usually three to four). *Without turning the needle, slide stitches to other end of needle, pull the yarn around the back, and knit the stitches as usual. Repeat from * for desired length.

Increases
Bar Increase Knitwise (k1f&b)

Knit into a stitch but leave it on the left needle **(Figure 1)**, then knit through the back loop of the same stitch **(Figure 2)** and slip the original stitch off the needle **(Figure 3)**.

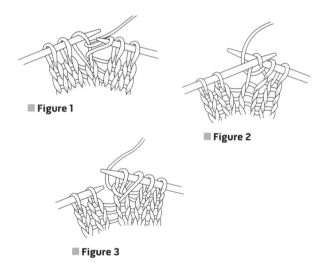

■ **Figure 1**

■ **Figure 2**

■ **Figure 3**

Bar Increase Purlwise (p1f&b)

Purl into a stitch but leave the stitch on the left needle **(Figure 1)**, then purl through the back loop of the same stitch **(Figure 2)** and slip the original stitch off the needle.

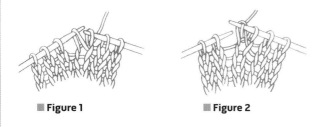

■ **Figure 1**   ■ **Figure 2**

Lifted Increase

RIGHT SLANT (RLI)

Knit into the back of the stitch (in the "purl bump") in the row directly below the stitch on the needle **(Figure 1)**, then knit the stitch on the needle **(Figure 2)**, and slip the original stitch off the needle.

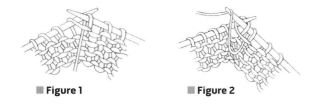

■ **Figure 1**   ■ **Figure 2**

LEFT SLANT (LLI)

Insert left needle tip into the back of the stitch below the stitch just knitted **(Figure 1)**, then knit this stitch **(Figure 2)**.

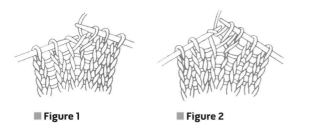

■ **Figure 1**   ■ **Figure 2**

Raised Make One

Note: Use the left slant if no direction of slant is specified.

LEFT SLANT (M1L)

With left needle tip, lift the strand between the last knitted stitch and the first stitch on the left needle from front to back **(Figure 1)**, then knit the lifted loop through the back **(Figure 2)**.

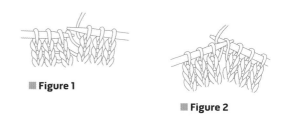

■ **Figure 1**

■ **Figure 2**

RIGHT SLANT (M1R)

With left needle tip, lift the strand between the needles from back to front **(Figure 1)**, then knit the lifted loop through the front **(Figure 2)**.

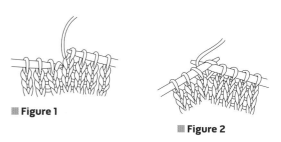

■ **Figure 1**

■ **Figure 2**

Seams

Horizontal-to-Horizontal Grafting

Working with the bound-off and cast-on edges opposite each other, right sides of the knitting facing you, and working into the stitches just below the bound-off and cast-on edges, bring threaded tapestry needle out at the center of the first stitch (i.e., go under half of the first stitch) on one side of the seam, then bring needle in and out under the first whole stitch on the other side **(Figure 1)**. *Bring needle into the center of the same stitch it came out of before, then out in the center of the adjacent stitch **(Figure 2)**. Bring needle in and out under the next whole stitch on the other side **(Figure 3)**. Repeat from *, ending with a half-stitch on the first side.

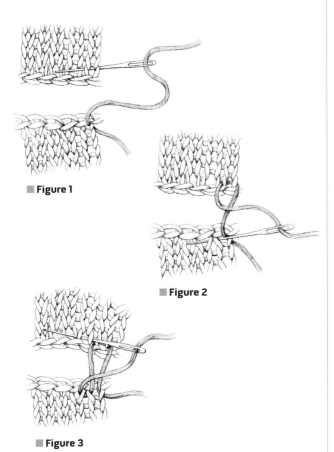

▓ **Figure 1**

▓ **Figure 2**

▓ **Figure 3**

Horizontal-to-Vertical Seam

With yarn threaded on a tapestry needle, pick up one bar between the first two stitches along the vertical edge **(Figure 1)**, then pick up one complete stitch along the horizontal edge **(Figure 2)**. *Pick up the next one or two bars (as needed for a flat seam) on the first piece, then the next whole stitch on the other piece **(Figure 3)**. Repeat from *, ending by picking up one bar on the vertical edge.

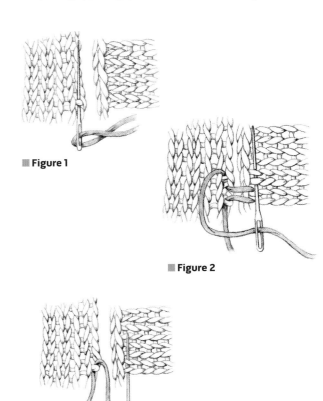

▓ **Figure 1**

▓ **Figure 2**

▓ **Figure 3**

Kitchener Stitch

Arrange stitches on two needles so that there is the same number of stitches on each needle. Hold the needles parallel to each other with wrong sides of the knitting together. Allowing about ½" (1.3 cm) per stitch to be grafted, thread matching yarn on a tapestry needle. Work from right to left as follows:

Step 1. Bring tapestry needle through the first stitch on the front needle as if to purl and leave the stitch on the needle **(Figure 1)**.

Step 2. Bring tapestry needle through the first stitch on the back needle as if to knit and leave that stitch on the needle **(Figure 2)**.

Step 3. Bring tapestry needle through the first front stitch as if to knit and slip this stitch off the needle, then bring tapestry needle through the next front stitch as if to purl and leave this stitch on the needle **(Figure 3)**.

Step 4. Bring tapestry needle through the first back stitch as if to purl and slip this stitch off the needle, then bring tapestry needle through the next back stitch as if to knit and leave this stitch on the needle **(Figure 4)**.

Repeat Steps 3 and 4 until one stitch remains on each needle, adjusting the tension to match the rest of the knitting as you go. To finish, bring tapestry needle through the front stitch as if to knit and slip this stitch off the needle, then bring tapestry needle through the back stitch as if to purl and slip this stitch off the needle.

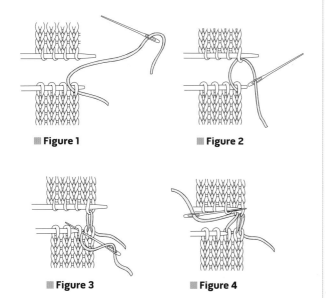

■ **Figure 1**   ■ **Figure 2**

■ **Figure 3**   ■ **Figure 4**

Mattress Stitch

Place the pieces to be seamed on a table, right sides facing up. Begin at the lower edge and work upward as follows for your stitch pattern:

STOCKINETTE STITCH WITH 1-STITCH SEAM ALLOWANCE

Insert threaded needle under one bar between the two edge stitches on one piece, then under the corresponding bar plus the bar above it on the other piece **(Figure 1)**. *Pick up the next two bars on the first piece **(Figure 2)**, then the next two bars on the other **(Figure 3)**. Repeat from *, ending by picking up the last bar or pair of bars on the first piece.

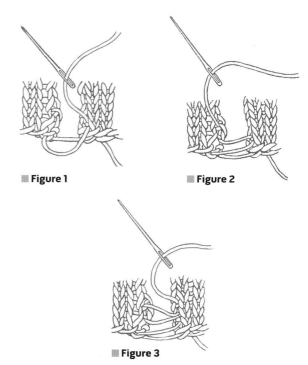

■ **Figure 1**   ■ **Figure 2**

■ **Figure 3**

STOCKINETTE STITCH WITH ½-STITCH SEAM ALLOWANCE

To reduce bulk in the mattress stitch seam, work as for the 1-stitch seam allowance but pick up the bars in the center of the edge stitches instead of between the last two stitches.

GARTER STITCH

*Insert threaded needle under the lower purl bar between the two edge stitches on one piece **(Figure 1)**, then the upper purl bar from the stitch next to the edge stitch on the same row of the other piece **(Figure 2)**. Repeat from *.

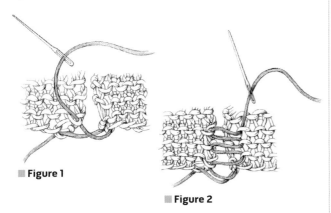

■ Figure 1

■ Figure 2

REVERSE STOCKINETTE STITCH

Working with the right sides of the knitting facing you, use the threaded needle to *pick up the lower purl bar between the last two stitches on one piece **(Figure 1)**, then the upper purl bar of the edge stitch on the other piece **(Figure 2)**. Repeat from *, always working in the lower purl bar on the first side and in the upper purl bar on the other.

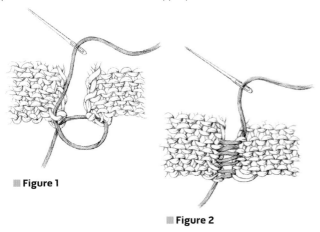

■ Figure 1

■ Figure 2

Slip-Stitch Crochet Seam

With wrong sides together and working one stitch at a time, *insert crochet hook through both thicknesses into the stitch just below the bound-off edge (or one stitch in from the selvedge edge), grab a loop of yarn and draw this loop through both thicknesses, then through the loop on the hook. Repeat from *, keeping even tension on the crochet stitches.

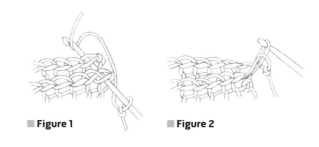

■ Figure 1   **■ Figure 2**

Whipstitch

Hold pieces to be sewn together so that the edges to be seamed are even with each other. With yarn threaded on a tapestry needle, *insert needle through both layers from back to front, then bring needle to back. Repeat from *, keeping even tension on the seaming yarn.

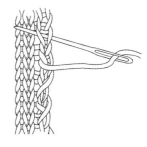

Short-Rows
Short-Rows Knit Side
Work to turning point, slip next stitch purlwise **(Figure 1)**, bring the yarn to the front, then slip the same stitch back to the left needle **(Figure 2)**, turn the work around and bring the yarn in position for the next stitch—one stitch has been wrapped and the yarn is correctly positioned to work the next stitch. When you come to a wrapped stitch on a subsequent row, hide the wrap by working it together with the wrapped stitch as follows: Insert right needle tip under the wrap (from the front if wrapped stitch is a knit stitch; from the back if wrapped stitch is a purl stitch; **Figure 3**), then into the stitch on the needle, and work the stitch and its wrap together as a single stitch.

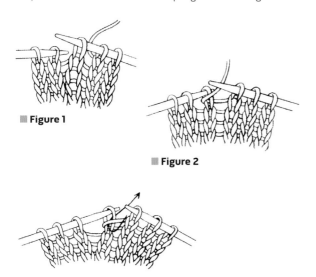

■ **Figure 1**

■ **Figure 2**

■ **Figure 3**

Short-Rows Purl Side
Work to the turning point, slip the next stitch purlwise to the right needle, bring the yarn to the back of the work **(Figure 1)**, return the slipped stitch to the left needle, bring the yarn to the front between the needles **(Figure 2)**, and turn the work so that the knit side is facing—one stitch has been wrapped, and the yarn is correctly positioned to knit the next stitch. To hide the wrap on a subsequent purl row, work to the wrapped stitch, use the tip of the right needle to pick up the wrap from the back, place it on the left needle **(Figure 3)**, then purl it together with the wrapped stitch.

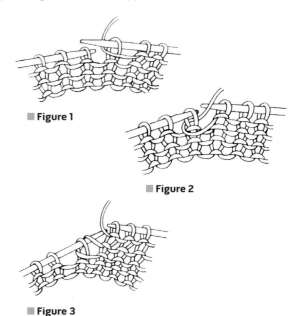

■ **Figure 1**

■ **Figure 2**

■ **Figure 3**

abbreviations

beg(s)	begin(s); beginning	**M1**	make one (increase)	**st(s)**	stitch(es)
BO	bind off	**p**	purl	**St st**	stockinette stitch
CC	contrasting color	**p1f&b**	purl into front and back of same stitch	**tbl**	through back loop
cm	centimeter(s)			**tog**	together
cn	cable needle	**patt(s)**	pattern(s)	**WS**	wrong side
CO	cast on	**psso**	pass slipped stitch over	**wyb**	with yarn in back
cont	continue(s); continuing	**pwise**	purlwise, as if to purl	**wyf**	with yarn in front
dec(s)	decrease(s); decreasing	**rem**	remain(s); remaining	**yd**	yard(s)
		rep	repeat(s); repeating	**yo**	yarnover
dpn	double-pointed needles	**rev St st**	reverse stockinette stitch	*****	repeat starting point
foll	follow(s); following	**rnd(s)**	round(s)	*** ***	repeat all instructions between asterisks
g	gram(s)	**RS**	right side		
inc(s)	increase(s); increasing	**sl**	slip	**( )**	alternate measurements and/or instructions
k	knit	**sl st**	slip st (slip 1 stitch purlwise unless otherwise indicated)		
k1f&b	knit into the front and back of same stitch			**[ ]**	work instructions as a group a specified number of times
kwise	knitwise, as if to knit	**ssk**	slip 2 stitches knitwise, one at a time, from the left needle to right needle, insert left needle tip through both front loops and knit together from this position (1 stitch decrease)		
m	marker(s)				
MC	main color				
mm	millimeter(s)				

sources for supplies

BERROCO INC.
PO Box 367
14 Elmdale Rd.
Uxbridge, MA 01569
berroco.com
in Canada: S. R. Kertzer Ltd.

BROWN SHEEP COMPANY
100662 County Rd. 16
Mitchell, NE 69357
brownsheep.com

CASCADE YARNS
PO Box 58168
1224 Andover Park E.
Tukwila, WA 98188
cascadeyarns.com

CRYSTAL PALACE YARNS
160 23rd St.
Richmond, CA 94804
straw.com/cpy

DIAMOND YARN
9697 St. Laurent, Ste. 101
Montréal, QC
Canada H3L 2N1
and
155 Martin Ross, Unit 3
Toronto, ON
Canada M3J 2L9
diamondyarn.com

S. R. KERTZER LTD.
50 Trowers Rd.
Woodbridge, ON
Canada L4L 7K6
kertzer.com

LOUET NORTH AMERICA
3425 Hands Rd.
Prescott, ON
Canada K0E 1T0
louet.com

PLYMOUTH YARN COMPANY
PO Box 28
Bristol, PA 19007
plymouthyarn.com

**SOUTH WEST TRADING
COMPANY**
918 S. Park Ln., Ste. 102
Tempe, AZ 85281
soysilk.com

TAHKI/STACY CHARLES INC.
70–30 80th St., Bldg. 36
Ridgewood, NY 11385
tahkistacycharles.com
in Canada: Diamond Yarn

MEUNCH YARNS/LANA GROSSA
1323 Scott St.
Petaluma, CA 94954
lanagrossa.com

**WESTMINSTER FIBERS
/ROWAN**
165 Ledge St.
Nashua, NH 03060
westminsterfibers.com
in Canada: Diamond Yarn

index

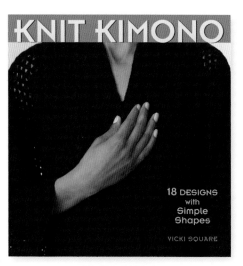
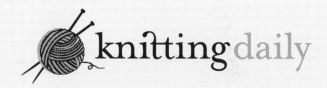